Loving Your Daughter-in-law

What *YOU* Can Do to Have a Better Relationship With Your Daughter-in-law

CHERYL OLIVER POLLOCK

Copyright © 2014 Cheryl Pollock.

All rights reserved. No part of this book may be used or reproduced by any means, graphic, electronic, or mechanical, including photocopying, recording, taping or by any information storage retrieval system without the written permission of the publisher except in the case of brief quotations embodied in critical articles and reviews.

Scriptures taken from the Holy Bible, New International Version®, NIV®. Copyright © 1973, 1978, 1984, 2011 by Biblica, Inc.™ Used by permission of Zondervan. All rights reserved worldwide. www.zondervan.com The "NIV" and "New International Version" are trademarks registered in the United States Patent and Trademark Office by Biblica, Inc.™ All rights reserved.

WestBow Press books may be ordered through booksellers or by contacting:

WestBow Press
A Division of Thomas Nelson & Zondervan
1663 Liberty Drive
Bloomington, IN 47403
www.westbowpress.com
1 (866) 928-1240

Because of the dynamic nature of the Internet, any web addresses or links contained in this book may have changed since publication and may no longer be valid. The views expressed in this work are solely those of the author and do not necessarily reflect the views of the publisher, and the publisher hereby disclaims any responsibility for them.

Any people depicted in stock imagery provided by Thinkstock are models, and such images are being used for illustrative purposes only. Certain stock imagery © Thinkstock.

ISBN: 978-1-4908-4779-5 (sc)
ISBN: 978-1-4908-4780-1 (hc)
ISBN: 978-1-4908-4778-8 (e)

Library of Congress Control Number: 2014914384

Printed in the United States of America.

WestBow Press rev. date: 08/27/2014

Contents

Acknowledgements iv
Preface vi
Introduction ix
Pretest xi

Part 1
Preparing to Become a Mother-in-law

Chapter 1　Biblical Preparation 2
Chapter 2　Practical Preparation for Becoming a
　　　　　　Mother-in-law 32
Chapter 3　He's Engaged! 55
Chapter 4　Keeping the Wedding from Becoming a
　　　　　　Nightmare 66

Part 2
Being a Prepared Mother-in-Law

Chapter 5　Those Newlyweds- The Early Years 94
Chapter 6　Did You Call Me Grandma? 124
Chapter 7　Over the Long Haul 150
Chapter 8　Now That We Are Friends 190
Chapter 9　When Nothing Seems to Work 217

Appendix 225

Acknowledgements

On my report card in elementary school, I am sure the box was checked, "Works and plays well with others," because the truth is that I work and play ***best*** when others are involved. There were certainly a lot of people involved in encouraging and assisting me in writing this book.

My profound gratitude goes to Kate and Don Balasa. It was Kate that had the idea to organize the book in chronological order. She also invested in this project by editing the manuscript. Don encouraged and prayed for me and contributed his advice and expertise any time it was needed.

I am thankful for my dear friends and Life Coaches, Kathy Alderson and Amy Leutke whose wise words and guidance gave me the confidence to keep writing. Other cheerleaders and prayer partners include Barb Condron, Marcia Furrow, Peggy Jane and Diann Hunt. Sandi Schwab and Monema Stephens did an incredible job in the final editing of the book. Ann Burdett was gracious to give her time and assistance as she distributed and collected surveys on the west coast. I am also very grateful to all of the ladies who shared their stories. Even though I can't include their names, I hope they know what a help they have been to many other women.

Then, there is my brother in Christ and pastor, Dan Weyerhaeuser. His teachings bleed through this entire book. Many of the concepts that I have written about, I adopted after hearing and pondering on his sermons. He has been more than generous in giving me permission to use some of his illustrations and quotes.

I am thankful for the gift of my family, for my parents, Gerald and Jewel Oliver and for my three sons who were wise enough to pick the wonderful girls they did so I could have them as daughters-in-law. Thank you, Christopher Pollock, Jonathan Pollock and Matthew Pollock. I am more appreciative than I will ever be able to say to my dear husband, Mark Pollock who happens to be the greatest man I know. He prayed, encouraged and made sacrifices for me so that I could fulfill my dream to write this book. After Jesus, he is the best thing that ever happened to me.

Finally, I am so grateful to God for saving me, loving me and directing me along this path in life. It has been sheer joy to walk with Him.

Preface

I am *not* the perfect mother-in-law, and I struggle because I want to be. I am not writing this book out of my wealth of wonderful, ideal experiences with my daughters-in-law. I don't do everything right, and we don't get along flawlessly all of the time. Sometimes I get on their nerves or I blurt out things that are intrusive or thoughtless. I *am* writing this because I love them dearly and long to have a great relationship with them. So, I have collected anecdotes and drawn upon the wisdom of some of the most incredible mothers-in-law that I know to give me ideas and strategies and to show me the way to having a great relationship with my daughters-in-law.

    I am the mother of three sons, and I couldn't wait to have daughters-in-law. Finally, after living with all of that testosterone, I would have someone who would "get" me. I would have someone with whom I could shop, talk, and yes, even cry, and those guys could just stand and stare as far as I was concerned because now I wasn't the *only* object of their confusion.

    Being a mother-in-law didn't come as naturally as I had hoped, however. In fact, I still have not achieved "mother-in-law of the year" status. I have found that striving to be the perfect mother-in-law is a misguided goal. It is something that I can never achieve and if I continue to pursue it, I will be constantly disappointed in myself or in my relationship with the girls. There has only been one perfect person, and He is the one encouraging me to quit trying to be Him. So if you are trying to be perfect, dear mother-in-law, leave that job to the only one who can be, and just pray that you will be the best mother-in-law that God can help you to be.

Concerning your daughter-in-law, it is unlikely that she wants to be as difficult as you are sometimes tempted to believe. Often contentious relationships come about from misconceptions, misunderstandings or horrible past experiences. In most cases, things are not hopeless. There are actions you can take to have a better relationship with your son's wife. Contained within the context of this book are many tools to help you improve that relationship. They are gathered and gleaned from some amazing mothers-in-law and it is my joy to share them with you.

Since I have only daughters-in-law, I am going to speak and write from that perspective. From my study and anecdotally it seems as though those are the most difficult relationships. (Girls, why do we do this to each other?) Don't put this book down, however, if you have sons-in-law. Many of the ideas and strategies included will work in a mother-in-law/son-in-law relationship as well.

I have arranged the chapters in chronological order that coincide with the stages of your son's life and your life as mother and mother-in-law. It begins when your son is a boy and progresses through his wedding to your new daughter-in-law, the birth of their children, and over the long haul of their marriage until death do you part. In so doing, I trust that you will more readily find the section that relates to your life now. Since it is written in chronological order, the lengths of the chapters vary. There seems to be more to say about some stages of life as a mother-in-law than others.

The information contained in this book is based on biblical principles. All scripture references are from the New International Version of the Bible unless otherwise indicated.

Many illustrations of real life examples are included within this book. I have been given permission to share them with you, but all names and a few incidental facts have been changed to protect the innocent from the guilty. I do want it to be as positive as possible, so you will find quotes throughout the chapters that include responses from women of every age about the best thing their mothers-in-law ever did for them or things that their mothers-in-law taught them. They are all from the daughter-in-law's point of view so that each quote can be another source of inspiration for mothers-in-law. I'm hoping these little inserts of upbeat sentences will spur your imagination and provide ideas that you can apply to your relationship with your daughter-in-law.

There is one additional note that I must add that is of the utmost importance. I am not a counselor. *This book is not for a toxic or emotionally sick relationship.* If that is the kind of situation that you find yourself in with your daughter-in-law, my suggestion is to find a reputable Christian counselor and go to him/her as quickly as possible. This book is for the mother-in-law that needs some inspiration or pointers on specific things that she can do or stop doing to enhance her relationship with her daughter-in-law.

So, Moms-in-law, hang on and let's ride this thing together and see if we can be the exception to the rule, and to all of those awful mother-in-law jokes.

Introduction

Momzilla or mother-in-law extraordinaire, which would I be?

The question percolated in my head the night I found myself in a small group of the most spiritually mature women in our church. Part of me wondered what in the world I was doing there. The other part decided that I would listen and learn. One woman in particular was known as a woman of prayer and great Bible knowledge. It was not unusual for her to spend eight hours a day studying the Bible or praying, so my ears always perked up when she spoke.

Sometime during the course of the evening I heard her mention her mother-in-law. What she said was not negative but there was something about the way she made her comment that made me ask the question that I thought had an obvious answer. After all, I knew the caliber of woman that she was. I blurted out my question, "You don't have a good relationship with your mother in law?" That godly woman looked me square in the eye and said with a straight face and sweet voice, "My mother-in-law is the anti-Christ!"

I was stunned, horrified and amused all at the same time. What in the world was this mother-in-law doing to deserve a characterization like that? My friend shared just a couple of sentences about the treatment that she had received from her mother-in-law and I continued to be amazed. It was then that I realized that her mother-in-law thought the same thing about her.

Because I had daughters-in-law and longed to have a good relationship with them, I was filled with curiosity and questions. Why wouldn't a mother-in-law do everything she possibly could to have a good relationship with the wife of her son? What does she gain by trying to hold onto her son to the detriment of his marriage and her relationship with his spouse, or worse, future grandchildren? Why does a mother-in-law think no one is good enough for her son? Why does a mother-in-law insist that her children do things her way? In other words, why would any mother-in-law sabotage a relationship that, hopefully, she is going to have until she dies?

One question led to another and another. Gradually, my questions started turning in direction. Does it have to be this way? Is it possible to have a loving, caring relationship with my daughters-in-law? Are there any examples of good mothers-in-law? Can I live my whole life as a mother-in-law and never be characterized as Cruella DeVil by my daughters-in-law? I wanted a great relationship, Ruth and Naomi style. They were the positive Biblical example that I aspired to emulate.

As a mother-in-law, I had to find the answers to these questions. I wanted then and continue to want to be a mother-in-law like Naomi (minus the bitterness part) to my three Ruths. And trust me, I don't want them, nor do I, want to be associated with the anti-Christ in any way.

Before you begin reading this book, take this pretest to see how well you know your daughter-in-law. You heard me. Test. It's ok. You can do it. Just give it a look and try your best.

Pretest

1. What is your daughter-in-law's full name? You think I'm kidding, don't you?
2. What is her birth date?
3. What is her favorite color?
4. What is her preferred decorating style?
5. How does she celebrate holidays?
6. What hobbies does she have?
7. What kind of relationship does she have with her mother, her father, her siblings?
8. What is her "love language?" Don't know what that is? It will be discussed in detail in Chapter 3.
9. What positive qualities do you see in her?
   And now the hardest question of all.........
10. What attracted your son to her?

Part 1

Preparing to Become a Mother-in-law

Chapter 1

Biblical Preparation

"Sons are a heritage from the Lord,
children a reward from Him."
(Psalm 127:3)

Memories of that day still hurt. Kristie was just happy to have a reason to celebrate. The last few years had been filled with so many difficulties for her and her husband that the strain was beginning to take a toll on their marriage. Her husband, Dave, had a degenerative back problem and suffered chronic pain, which only allowed him to work intermittently. Kristie also had been dealing with ongoing physical problems that sent their combined medical bills skyrocketing into the tens of thousands. By the grace of God, she was able to work and do her best to help support them, but things were extremely tight financially.

But today they wouldn't think about those things. Today was Dave's birthday, and Kristie was determined to make it special. Dave's mother had flown in from out of state, and tonight they would have a celebration. Kristie had awakened early to begin preparations for the party. She got a boxed mix out of her cabinet, baked a cake, and then carefully frosted and decorated it. She left it out on the counter so that Dave would be sure to see it. After a few finishing touches, Kristie rushed off to work, happy that she had finished the cake and imagining the look on Dave's face when he found it. Hopefully that little birthday surprise would lift his spirits.

After a long workday, Kristie came home weary but excited to celebrate her husband's birthday. When she walked into the kitchen, she was surprised to find that the cake she had gotten up early to prepare had been replaced by a store-bought one. She looked around the kitchen and was horrified to find her cake in the trash! Had there been some accident? Had it inadvertently been dropped or knocked off the counter?

When her mother-in-law came into the room, Kristie asked her what had happened. Her mother-in-law explained she had seen the box for the mix in the trash and had noticed it was past the expiration date, so she had thrown the cake away and bought a good one! Kristie couldn't believe it. She was embarrassed, angry and devastated. Yes, it still hurts when she remembers that day.

Why would anyone be that thoughtless and callous? What was Kristie's mother-in-law trying to accomplish? Was she trying to prove she could provide the better cake? Was this a power play or was she trying to save her sweet, innocent son from being poisoned by a daughter-in-law who didn't know anything? Was she trying to show her superior knowledge about all things baked, or was her action a subtle message to her daughter-in-law about her "place"? Seriously, has anyone ever died from eating an expired cake mix? I doubt it. But, people's spirits have died from the thoughtless words and actions of others. You don't have to take a Dale Carnegie course to know that this is no way to "win friends and influence people". This is a prime example of why mothers-in-law get their bad reputation.

There is the possibility that Kristie's mother-in-law just didn't think when she threw away Kristie's cake and replaced it with another. My message throughout this book is that mothers-in-law *have to think*. If we want good and loving relationships with our daughters-in-law, and later, with our grandchildren, we *must* think before we say or do things.

We also need to keep in mind that we are not the only two at play in this relationship. We have an Enemy who wants to destroy us, and he also wants to destroy all our relationships. We certainly do not want to be Satan's accomplices. You may think it sounds a little bizarre to accept the idea that we have an adversary, but consider what the Bible says in John 10:10 about this enemy: "The thief [Satan] comes only to steal and kill and destroy; I [Jesus] have come that they might have life and have it to the full." In 1 Peter 5:8, the Bible tells us, "Your enemy the devil prowls around like a roaring lion looking for someone to devour." Why? Satan wants to be God. Since he cannot, he loathes Him and everything loved by God. In his rage and hatred, Satan has systematically set out to destroy everything that God loves. Everything. That includes you and me and, believe it or not, our relationships.

He has obviously had some success, because there is no relationship more consistently antagonistic than that between a mother-in-law and daughter-in-law. Even conventional wisdom and pop culture confirm that fact. Google "mother-in-law jokes," and you will be amazed at what pops up.

Do we mothers-in-law *have* to get swallowed up in the same old trap in which millions of other mothers-in-law have been caught? Are we destined to be the butt of jokes and the subject of whispers and gossip? Do we have to live out the rest of our lives with heartache and distance between our sons' families and us? Is there any source that we can look to in order to find real help to break this destructive cycle? Is there any way to fight this Enemy who is purposely trying to sabotage our relationship with our daughters-in-law? The good news is that there is and we are going to look to that source.

I know you are anxious to get right to the practical help and to the list of concrete tools you can implement to enhance your relationship with your daughter-in-law. It is important, however, to build anything that we do on a firm foundation. That foundation is the Word of God, the Bible. So let's begin there and lay down some biblical groundwork on which to build as we prepare to be the best mothers-in-law possible. We will get to the application of these principles in chapter 3.

The best thing my mother-in-law ever did for me was raise an awesome son!
—Anonymous

Meddling Mama

We don't have to look far into the Bible to find a mother-in-law/daughter-in-law relationship. The first such relationship is at the beginning, in the book of Genesis. This story starts with the patriarch of the Jewish people, Abraham. God promises Abraham that He will make him into a great nation and that all the peoples of the earth will be blessed through him and the son that God will give him. That son, Isaac, is finally born to Abraham in his old age. Because Isaac is a child of promise, Abraham doesn't want just any wife for him when he becomes an adult. He sends his most trusted servant to go back to his homeland and handpick a wife for this special son. That servant finds Rebekah, a woman from Abraham's own people.

By the providence and grace of God, Isaac and Rebekah are married and have twin sons. The oldest is named Esau and becomes his daddy's favorite. The second of the twins to be born is Jacob who becomes his mommy's fave. It sounds like trouble already, doesn't it? Having favorites never comes to any good.

The boys become men and when they are forty years old, Esau gets married. Finally we come to the part in the narrative that includes a mother-in-law/daughter-in-law relationship. Maybe we can get some ideas and helpful hints on being a great mother-in-law from Rebekah. But wait. Genesis 26:34-35 says, "When Esau was forty years old, he married Judith daughter of Berri the Hittite, and also Basemath daughter of Elon the Hittite. *They were a source of grief to Isaac and Rebekah."* (emphasis added)

Slam on the brakes! This is definitely *not* what we want to hear. First Rebekah had to adjust to *two* daughters-in-law after having her boys to herself for forty years. Second, those girls were a source of grief? Let's keep reading. There has to be something that can be learned from Rebekah and her relationship with her daughters-in-law. As we continue, however, we find that the things to be learned from Rebekah are *not* what we want to emulate or reproduce in our relationships with our daughters-in-law.

Some of the great things my mother-in-law has done for me are: First, [she] prays for us, especially my girls, whom she adores. Second, she loves my girls and is a wonderful grandmother to them. Third, she raised my husband to be a man of integrity and trained him to do little things like put the toilet seat down, help

me with dishes, etc. Fourth, I have really appreciated her taking care of our girls so [my husband] and I could get away alone from time to time.
—Anonymous

Cutting Off Her Nose to Spite Her Face

In the very next chapter of Genesis, there is an incredible account of how Rebekah masterminded a conspiracy that pitted her favorite son, Jacob, against her less favored son, Esau. It was her plan to steal from her husband and their father the most valuable gift that Esau could ever hope to inherit. That gift was the blessing that Isaac planned and prepared to give to Esau. Through Rebekah and Jacob's conniving and deception, they managed to trick Isaac into giving the blessing to Jacob instead. This was no small matter. The blessing had legal implications that were binding until death. The IVP New Bible Dictionary says, "The Old Testament lays great stress on the blessing of Patriarchs to their children. For example, Isaac cannot reverse what he has promised to Jacob (Genesis 27:33, 37). The Bible does not visualize anyone's pronouncing an effective blessing contrary to God's will. The Patriarchs believe that God is showing them the future of their descendants, and their blessing is declaratory of this." No matter how much he wanted to, Isaac's blessing to Jacob, even under nefarious circumstances, was unbreakable. There was very little left for Esau.

Esau's blessing rightfully belonged to the oldest son in the family, but tradition and rights were inconsequential to Rebekah. What mattered to her was that she got what she wanted for Jacob. She had big dreams for him that did not include Esau. Her dreams were so big that she was willing to take a curse upon herself if they got caught in the act of their deception. (Genesis 27:13) Her meddling resulted in a cascade of negative events, some of which are still felt to this day.

The dominos started to tumble. The first fell when Jacob had to flee for his life after stealing Esau's blessing. Esau was so filled with rage that he literally wanted to kill his brother. Can you imagine the angst and horror it would cause if one of your children actually wanted to murder another of your children because of something that you instigated?

The best thing that my mother-in-law ever did for me was compliment me on being a good mother!
—Anonymous

Rebekah's Reckoning

Another tragic result of Rebekah's duplicity is that scripture implies she never got to see her favorite son again. He ran away to Rebekah's childhood home in Northwest Mesopotamia where he stayed for many years. Jacob married two of Rebekah's nieces, Leah and Rachel, but Rebekah never got to experience the joy of a relationship with daughters-in-law of which she probably would have approved. She lost out on the opportunity to rock her grandbabies from her favorite son, Jacob, or pass on skills, talents and traditions that had been handed down to her. She never got to pray with them or tell them stories about their daddy's childhood. She could only dream about the things that grandmas love to do with their loved grandchildren. The very things that Rebekah likely longed for, she missed out on because of her own sin.

Rebekah was left back home with daughters-in-law that "were a source of grief" to her and Isaac. Ironically, what happened to Rebekah was that she, as my grandmother would say, "Cut off her nose to spite her face." Her conniving ended up biting her right in the backside because the daughters-in-law she was left with gave her a pain in the same place.

The last sad outcome from Rebekah and Jacob's deception is recorded in Genesis 28:6-9. "Now Esau learned that Isaac had blessed Jacob and had sent him to Paddan Aram to take a wife from there, and that when he blessed him he commanded him, 'Do not marry a Canaanite woman,' and that Jacob had obeyed his father and mother and had gone to Paddan Aram. Esau then realized how displeasing the Canaanite women were to his father Isaac; so he went to Ishmael and married Mahalath sister of Nebaioth, the daughter of Ishmael son of Abraham, in addition to the wives the already had."

After everything that had happened to Esau, he still wanted the approval of his parents. Since her less favored son had married a third wife, Rebekah now had another daughter-in-law with which to contend. One wonders if she got along any better with that one than the first two.

Is there anything to be learned about being a loving, godly mother-in-law from Rebekah's example? Her account is more an illustration of what *not* to do. We do learn some important lessons, however.

We learn that:

- Favoritism destroys relationships within a family.
- Sinful, selfish meddling in your grown children's affairs is detrimental to all.

- Conspiring against your husband is wrong and it is displeasing to God. It can damage your marriage and the peace in your home.
- Even adult children want the approval of their parents.
- Sin has long-lasting consequences.

We will discuss these issues and how they affect the relationship that we have with our daughters-in-law at greater length later in this book. Notice that Rebekah's meddling, her conspiring to deceive her husband, and her sin were all bound up together. One wrong decision led to another and another until the whole situation snowballed out of control.

Knowing that now and remembering it in the moment, however, are two different things. Sometimes the temptation to get what we want or have our own way is so strong that we forget the terrible ramifications of sin.

When struggling with sin, there is a word picture that I play on the screen of my mind that has helped me when I allow it. I picture a figure that looks beautiful at a glance beckoning me and wooing me, saying, "Come on. You are going to love this. How can something that feels so right, be wrong? This is going to be even better than what you thought or dreamed." Then in my mind's eye I give in and succumb to the beautiful, soothing voice and do the very thing that, intellectually and spiritually, I know I shouldn't do; the thing that I know is a sin according to God's word. *Smack!* The second I do it, that beautiful face turns horrid and grotesque! That figure then stomps on me and laughs and says in a horrifying voice, "You weakling! I knew you would give in. What kind of Christian are you, anyway? Your God is going to be so disappointed in you. You might as well give up now."

If in the moment of temptation I can pray and draw on that word picture and see the deception of evil, the Holy Spirit strengthens me and, when I let Him, He enables me to resist that sin which I am being tempted to commit. How different would our world be now if Rebekah had resisted the temptation to deceive her husband?

I imagine that Rebekah was easily wooed into the sin of deception because of her own selfishness and her ambitious plans for her favorite son. She wanted to believe that it would all work out. She had convinced herself that the plan to steal Esau's blessing really was a good idea and better for the family and for everyone involved. She was duped and didn't realize that the enemy was standing ready to stomp on her and on all of the great plans she had for Jacob. He demolished in one fell swoop any hopes and dreams that she ever had of having a relationship with her daughters-in-law and grandchildren from the favored son. She not only deceived Isaac, she deceived herself as well.

My [mother-in-law] never, ever criticized my parenting and I know that I sometimes did not do my best in front of her. She also always was relaxed and comfortable when we were visiting. Therefore, I was always comfortable and relaxed even when the kids were making a mess.
—Anonymous

Rebekah's Legacy

Rebekah's conspiracy with Jacob to lie to her husband and steal from her son, Esau, caused such enmity between her sons that Esau wanted to kill Jacob. The only thing that kept him from succeeding was that Jacob fled for his life. Her sin fueled further sin committed by both of her sons.

In the centuries to follow these two boys' descendants became two separate nations. Jacob's family became the nation of Israel and Esau's became the people known as the Edomites. Wars, hatred and fighting have characterized these two people groups down through the millennia. The contention continues today as the Jewish nation of Israel and the Arab nations that surround her try and often fail to peacefully coexist. They have definitely not turned out to be kissing cousins. Rebekah's legacy became one of meddling, conspiracy, deceit, and sin. That is not the legacy that I want to leave my sons, daughters-in-law and grandchildren. What kind of legacy do you want to leave to those who follow you?

Rebekah's example shows us that the way we conduct ourselves with our husband and children really matters. We cannot rationalize that the little deceptions we try to pull over on our husbands are inconsequential. Every sin has repercussions and sometimes those repercussions last into the ensuing generations.

The best thing my mother-in-law ever did for me was model a positive outlook.
—Anonymous

I Would Never Be Deceptive Like Rebekah.......Would I?

I'm tempted to think that Rebekah was horrible in deceiving Isaac and that I would never participate in anything even remotely close to what she did. Then I remembered the outfit that I purchased. I remembered how I hung it in my closet and tucked the tag in so that my husband wouldn't see it and realize that the article of clothing was new. My unspoken motto had always been," If the tag doesn't show, he'll never know." That new item of clothing could remain hidden there smashed in among all my other clothes until an appropriate time to pull it out and wear it. The period of time was usually long enough that, if asked, I could say to him, "No. This is not new. I have had this for a while!"

Busted! Deception! By doing these and other "little" things, I am modeling in front of my children that it is ok to deceive. I am telling them by my actions that this is what wives do. I am teaching my sons that if they are not alert and watchful, their wives will do the same to them. By my little, tiny deceptions that "don't mean much," I am sowing in my sons seeds of distrust in the wives that they are yet to meet.

If I want them to be completely honest and God-honoring in their future relationships, I must live honestly in front of them with consistency. When they are begging for the McDonalds hamburgers that I don't want them to have, I can't say to them, "Sorry honey. McDonalds is out of hamburgers today." I have to tell the truth and deal with their, shall we say, negative reaction. When someone calls our home that I don't want to talk to, I cannot instruct my children to tell the person that, "Mommy is not home." They are learning from me how genuine believers in Jesus Christ conduct themselves. And, they are learning by watching me how godly wives conduct themselves. Wow! Maybe there are a few things that we can learn from Rebekah even if we have to learn them from the negative point of view. Whew! All of this intrigue has worn me out!

The best things that my mother-in-law ever did for me was be a great host, good listener and generous with our kids.
—Anonymous

A Modern Day Success Story

My oldest son, Chris, called me from college one day with a message unlike any he had ever had for me before. He wanted me to come to the campus and meet a girl that he was interested in and take her to lunch. It would be just Holly and me. He wanted to know if I liked this girl because he really did. I was thrilled that he would trust my judgment and want my approval. That should not have been a surprise to me. We have seen even from our brief look at Rebekah and her sons that Esau was willing to marry a third wife just to get his parents' approval. Now that's what I call going just a little bit too far! Things haven't changed that much over the centuries, though, because Christopher wanted my approval as well.

I had known Holly's family and knew they were wonderful Christian people, but I wanted to see for myself what Holly was like. Would I be able to tell within a few minutes at lunchtime if she was right for my son? Would I be able to get a read on her character and what she really thought of Christopher?

I remember that day vividly. I sat across the table from this beautiful, confident girl. She did not seem to be intimidated by me because I was older and "his" mother nor did she act nervous as we visited. She had the rare mix of self-assurance and respect. She struck just the right tone. We weren't but a few minutes into our conversation when I *knew* that I was looking eyeball to eyeball with my son's future wife and the girl for whom I had been praying for years. I was staring at an answer to my prayers. We hit it off almost from the minute we sat down.

I have since learned why Holly was so comfortable and confident that day at lunch. Holly's mother, Linda absolutely loved her own mother-in-law and often spoke of her deep devotion to her. Their relationship mimicked the positive biblical mother-in-law/daughter-in-law bond of Naomi and Ruth. We will be looking at that example from scripture in just a bit. Holly's paradigm when it came to the mother-in-law relationship was that of a loving, caring fondness between a mother-in-law and her daughter-in-law. She was not "set up" to dislike me or see me as an adversary. Holly came to that lunch with the expectation that she would like me and that we would get along well and that is exactly what happened.

One of the greatest gifts my girls' mothers have given them is the gift of positive, loving relationships with their own mothers-in-law, habitually modeling kindness and respect toward them. In so doing, their mothers set my daughters-in-law up for success with their future mother-in-law, me. I learned a huge lesson from how the girls were raised. Loving and treating your own mother-in-law with respect is one of the best things you can do for your daughter's future relationship with her mother-in-law.

The best thing my mother-in-law ever did for me was to build me up, compliment me and always convey God's love for me through her life. She was an amazing, Godly woman, who in spite of ovarian cancer, kept a positive attitude and always left everything in God's hands. The one big thing that she

always did was take my side whenever my husband and I would have disagreements. She loved me like a daughter. I was very, very blessed to be able to live with her daily for the last six years of her life.
—Anonymous

An Ancient Success Story

So you just read a modern day example of a positive mother-in-law/daughter-in-law relationship, but surely there has to be a more constructive biblical example of this kind of relationship than we saw in Rebekah and her daughters-in-law. I know. I can hear you yelling at me. "What about Ruth and Naomi?" Aren't you thankful that they are in scripture? It was starting to get discouraging as we yearned for a positive role model from the Bible. However, lest you think that just everything was perfect for them, let me give you a quick synopsis of what was going on in their lives.

Naomi and her husband, Elimelech, were Israelites descended from Rebekah's favorite twin, Jacob. They lived with their two sons in Bethlehem until it was overtaken by a famine. They were so desperate that they left their home in Bethlehem and went to the foreign country of Moab to get food. This was a pretty radical move because Israel and Moab had long been at odds.

While living in Moab, Elimelech died and left Naomi a single mother with two sons. Both of the boys married Moabite women, whose names were Orpah and Ruth. Not so good. God's word had instructed the Israelites over and over not to intermarry with people from other nations. I am only guessing, but I think it is pretty safe to say that these girls were probably not Naomi's idea of perfect matches for her sons. Orpah and Ruth were Gentiles from a pagan nation that served a pagan god. I would surmise that her ideal choice would have been two nice Jewish girls from the land of Judah just like herself. Despite the fact that her daughters-in-law may not have been the girls she had always dreamed about for her sons, she must have engendered true love from them. She must have loved them unconditionally to have them later show her so much love in return.

Also notice in Ruth 1:4 and 5 that both sons were married for 10 years, and their wives, Orpah and Ruth, did not produce any grandchildren for Naomi. Take it from this contemporary American grandmother; that would be a real disappointment. It would have been even more drastic in those days when it was the responsibility of the children and grandchildren to care for their elders. They were one's social security and retirement-plan all rolled into one.

Barrenness continues to be a problem within family structures in some cultures today. My middle son, Jon and his wife, Bekah live in the African country of Ethiopia where both serve as missionaries. My daughter-in-law, Bekah made a keen observation concerning that culture and child bearing. She shared with me that many men leave their wives if those wives can't produce children for them. It is not unusual for a man to leave even if his wife has given birth to two, three or four babies and then stops getting pregnant. I witnessed for myself the heartache of one woman who walked two and one half hours to the hospital to have, and try to save, her twenty-first baby. Only one of her children had survived. She was desperate to have another living child. Unfortunately, it didn't look like this baby was going to make it either. As Bekah and I were discussing this portion of scripture one day she mused that in some cultures today there is still incredible pressure from parents and grandparents to keep bearing those children. Hopefully, we know better than to do that. Let's get back to Naomi.

After 10 years, both of Naomi's sons died and left her a widow, childless, and even without grandchildren. All she had left were her two foreign daughters-in-law. That may sound like a nightmare to some of you, but an even bigger nightmare for Naomi was facing the future without those beloved girls. Yet, Naomi was selfless even in her despair. She cared more about the future of her daughters-in-law than her own. Naomi knew that she had nothing to offer the girls but poverty and a grueling journey back to Bethlehem. There was also the high probability that her daughters-in-law would not be accepted once they arrived in Naomi's homeland because they were foreigners. She loved them so much that she was willing to face the difficult future alone for their sakes. In Ruth 1:9 Naomi tells the girls, "'May the LORD grant that each of you will find rest in the home of another husband.' Then she kissed them goodbye and they wept aloud." She loved them enough to let them go at great cost to herself because that was what was best for them. She even verbally set them free to marry again. Out of her deep love for them, she encouraged them to go back to their own people and try to make a life for themselves.

Do your children see you trusting God and His sovereignty even through difficult events in your life? Or do they see you panic, curse God, get mad, quit attending church, or run to substances to help you "deal" with difficulties?

Katelyn had grown up going to church. Her parents were involved in the activities of the church and her father taught Sunday School. When Katelyn got into high school, however, things in her family turned upside down. Her mother began having an affair and her father became so hurt and frustrated about the situation that he decided he might as well do the same. When lovingly confronted with the wrong in their lives and the havoc that they were wreaking on their family, Katelyn's parents got mad and quit going to church altogether. Katelyn chose to do things differently. She stuck to her faith in Christ and stayed with what she knew to be right despite the actions of her family. Ultimately her parents were divorced. Through the grace of God her father came back to faith, but her mother went from one bad choice to the next.

Katelyn eventually married a guy from the church youth group that loved Jesus as much as she did. They were determined to have a different kind of marriage than her parents. Her new in-laws were people of character and integrity and Katelyn found she could count on them to be the role models that she desperately needed.

Through the years, while her own mother continued to spin out of control, Katelyn looked to her mother-in-law, Nancy, to show her how to deal with life's difficulties. Katelyn watched as Nancy experienced the death of both of her parents, Nancy's sister's breast cancer, four miscarried grandchildren, Nancy's husband's lung cancer and a bout with a debilitating auto-immune disease. No matter the circumstances in Nancy's life, she always drew upon her deep faith in a loving God and the truth of what God says in His word, that true joy comes when one is in a close relationship with God. Nancy, like Naomi, understood the sovereignty of God and that He can work even the bad things in life together to accomplish His plan, which is always good. Also like Naomi, Nancy was an example of how a mother-in-law can show dependence upon the Lord in speech and actions despite circumstances.

> *The best thing my mother-in-law ever did for me was write me a letter and let me know how thankful she was that her son married me and that I am the best person he could have married.*
> —Anonymous

Orpah Leaves and Ruth Cleaves

Orpah took Naomi's advice, but Ruth refused to leave the mother-in-law that she loved so deeply. This decision was a complete act of devotion. By this expression of unconditional love, Ruth was forever cutting all ties with her home, her country, the religion in which she was raised and, as far as she knew, she was giving up all prospects of ever marrying again. That choice had lifelong implications for Ruth and eternal implications for the rest of us. We discover later that because she chose to stay with Naomi and identify with her people and her God, Ruth ended up becoming the grandmother of King David and an ancestor to the Lord Jesus Christ! What she thought she was giving up was returned to her many times over. Read the rest of the book of Ruth from the Bible and you will be witness to the tender love story of Ruth and Boaz, whom she later met, and of God and the people that He loves.

But we return to the narrative before any of those wonderful things happen to Ruth and Naomi. It is not hard to notice that Naomi is a much better example of a mother-in-law than Rebekah. One of the incredible things that we see in Naomi is that she consistently acknowledged God's sovereign control despite her circumstances. In Ruth 1:6 it says, "When Naomi heard in Moab that *the LORD* (emphasis added) had come to the aid of his people by providing food for them, she and her daughters-in-law prepared to return home from there." She knew that God was sovereign over everything that happened to her and she openly shared this faith with her daughters-in-law. In verse 8, when Naomi was trying to persuade her daughters-in-law to go back home, she said, "May *the LORD* show you kindness, as you have shown kindness to your dead husbands and to me." Then when the younger ladies insisted on staying with Naomi, she said in verse 13b, "No, my daughters. It is more bitter for me than for you, *because the LORD's* hand has turned against me!" Four more times in this first chapter alone Naomi talks about even the hard things coming to her from the LORD. She had a firm understanding of the fact that God is sovereign over good events and bad and works all of them for His purpose.

Can you relate to the tug of war that goes on in the heart of a mom to let your grown children go, let them move on without you, let them make mistakes, let them choose what they think is best for them even when their plans don't include you? Can you relate to letting go of your hopes and dreams for your son so that he can live out his own?

I have wrestled at this very point. My son has said since he was a little boy that he was going to be a medical missionary. I was filled with joy and pride that Jon would want to serve God in that way. There were no worries because that seemed like years into the future. He majored in pre-med in college and was married a couple of months after graduation to my wonderful daughter-in-law, Bekah, who was the perfect complement and companion to Jon.

I first took notice of Bekah when she was just 15 years old. I was volunteering with the church youth group and she caught my attention right away. She had unusual spiritual maturity, as well as a bright mind and, oh yeah, she happened to be beautiful too. By the providence of God, Bekah had a deep desire to be a missionary just like Jon. Her mother, Renea and I knew that our kids would be perfect for each other, but we had to wait until they figured it out. To our joy, they began dating and finally married.

After they were married, it still didn't concern me too much that they would be going far away because of all of the schooling and training that Jon still had to do. Medical school flew by and then he went to Emory University Hospital in Atlanta to do his residency. No sweat. He still had five years of residency and then had to practice for a year to get some experience before he could go overseas. But, two years ago, Jon, Bekah and our two beautiful little granddaughters flew off to Ethiopia to begin their ministry. Ethiopia? Isn't that right between the Sudan and Somalia? Did they have to pick such a dangerous place? Maybe we should talk some sense into their heads.

How could it have gotten here so quickly? As they departed for their new home I began having a war in my spirit about Jon and Bekah leaving and going to an unsafe place to raise my granddaughters. What grandmother wouldn't be worried about that? Were my granddaughters going to grow up even knowing me? How was I going to "let them go?" It didn't take me long to realize that whether I "let them go" or not, they were going. God gently started speaking to my spirit and impressed me with the question, "Am I sovereign in Ethiopia just like I am in the United States?" "Yes Lord. You are sovereign there too" was, of course, my only sound response. "Would you rather have them here with you not being obedient to Me or in Ethiopia serving Me and being obedient to Me?" It didn't take me long to pick the latter. "OK, God. I pick there." I came to realize that the "letting go" part was for my benefit and their blessing. I was loosening my impotent grip on them and placing them in the ever-competent grip of Almighty God instead. That is a pretty good trade off.

My letting go was also for them. Either way they were going, but knowing they had the blessing of their parents has removed many road-blocks and obstacles from their way. It has made the journey for them joyous instead of contentious. They feel the freedom to come to us for advice, prayer and encouragement instead of avoiding us because the conversations may lead to arguments or ugly confrontations.

The quote by Richard Bach is true. "If you love something set it free. If it comes back, it was and always will be yours. If it never returns, it never was yours to begin with." Naomi set her daughters-in-law free, knowing the cost would be that she would be alone. She did it because she felt that was what was best for them. She set her own wants, desires and self-interest aside for the good of Orpah and Ruth. She received Ruth back and much, much more. She became an ancestor of the Messiah! Will you trust God and pry your fingers loose of your son and your daughter-in-law? It will mean freedom for you and could mean great blessing for you all.

The best thing that my mother-in-law ever did for me was raise my husband to know God.
—Anonymous

You're Marrying WHOM?

Mary was heartsick when her son, Kevin, who was barely old enough to vote, married Kari, who was nearly past childbearing years. Even more than the age difference, was the realization that both of them seemed to be drifting away from God rather than to Him. Despite the fact that this was not the match she would have made for her son, Mary was determined to love both of them and be the best mother-in-law that she could be to her daughter-in-law that was nearly her peer. Through some very difficult experiences in Kevin and Kari's lives, Mary has been able to demonstrate that love and become a real friend to her daughter-in-law, but it hasn't been easy. It has taken years of prayer and patience as Mary worked to establish trust with her daughter-in-law.

    I can only imagine what it must be like when your son falls in love with a girl that you really don't like or that you deem unsuitable in some way. The disappointment and heartache have to be overwhelming. This topic and what to do about it will be discussed further in the chapter entitled "The Engagement." For now it is helpful for us to look again at the biblical example of Naomi.

    Had you ever considered that Orpah and Ruth may not have been whom Naomi would have chosen for daughters-in-law? After all, they were foreign women, which made them unclean to a Jew, and their people worshiped pagan gods. It was strictly forbidden in the law for Jews to intermarry with non-Jews. These two girls represented everything that a good, Jewish mother tried to prevent her sons from becoming attached to. Yet, they became her beloved daughters-in-law. What happened to bring about this good relationship out of shaky circumstances?

    We can only guess what Naomi's initial feelings were toward Orpah and Ruth based on what we know about Jewish law and customs. This we know for sure; no matter how their relationship began, it is evident by Naomi's selflessness and concern for the girls that she ended up loving them dearly.

Once our sons are married, the deal is done. We, as mothers-in-law, need to do everything that we can to follow the example of Naomi and love our daughters-in-law unconditionally. I know what you are thinking. But what if she is of another faith? What if she is from a different culture? What if she is of a different race? What if she is physically handicapped? Is barren? Is uneducated? Has a lot more education than we do? Is from a different socio-economic background? What happens if she is shy and we are outgoing or if she is loud and boisterous and we are refined? What if she is confrontational and always in our face or what do we do if she is mousy and we can't get her to voice any opinion? When we are disappointed in his choice, how can we love her unconditionally? There is a wonderful pattern in Romans 12:9-21 that we can follow that, with God's help, will get us on the road to loving our daughters-in-law.

Romans 12:9 and 10 say that "Love must be sincere. Hate what is evil; cling to what is good. Be devoted to one another in love. Honor one another above yourselves." Ask God to give you a sincere love for your daughter-in-law. Ask Him to help you put her needs above your own. This can only be done through prayer and the work of the Holy Spirit in your life. He has the power to change her or change your heart. Tell Him how you feel and ask Him to give you His love for your daughter-in-law.

Romans 12:12 further instructs us to, "Be joyful in hope, patient in affliction, faithful in prayer." Three aspects of the fruit of the Spirit are mentioned in this verse; joy, patience and faithfulness. When we display these qualities, especially in the face of hostility, it is counter to everything in this world. Your daughter-in-law will notice because no person can exhibit behaviors like that on her own. It takes an all-powerful God to do that in you.

Verse 13 encourages us to "practice hospitality." Be hospitable to your son and daughter-in-law. Always welcome them with open arms. Make your home a safe, warm place to visit. One way of practicing hospitality is to talk about things in which your daughter-in-law is interested. Pay attention to her and what is going on in her life without being nosey. Be upbeat and encouraging, which leads to the next verse in Romans 12, "Bless those who persecute you; bless and do not curse." Never say a bad word about her or to her. Make your words those of blessing and up-building.

The text continues to verse 17 which says, "Do not repay anyone evil for evil." Have you noticed how easy it is to mimic the attitude of those around you? I can go to a restaurant and if I have a server that is impolite or snippy, I find that I am tempted to respond in the same way. It is even easier to do this to someone whom I have a difficult time loving. The scripture warns us not to get caught in that trap. God calls believers to react in the opposite way the world reacts. This requires the hard work of prayer, but God can help us to respond in His way. And talk about opposite world....He goes on to tell us in verses 20 and 21 that if our enemy is hungry or thirsty, we are to give her food and drink. We are not to "be overcome by evil, but overcome evil with good." This all sounds so difficult. In fact, it sounds impossible. God is not surprised that we can't pull this off on our own. He knows that we can't. He wants us to depend on Him. He does not command us to do anything that He cannot do through us. This kind of transformation requires us to be totally dependent upon Him.

If you have a daughter-in-law who would not have been your choice, read and pray and even memorize Romans 12. Ask God to love this girl through you. He can turn any relationship around.

If it never becomes the type of relationship that you long for, however, the victory in this situation will be you clinging to Christ.

The best thing my mother-in-law ever did for me was accept me as her daughter and treat me like one of her own children. [She] forgave me when I said a careless word. [She] came to the house for several days to take care of our three children so that [my husband] and I could have an extended trip to Europe for our belated 10th anniversary. I think that taking the grandkids so that the parents can get away alone together for a trip is a HUGE blessing!
—*Anonymous*

To Speak or Not to Speak, That is the Question

One of the things that I learned from Naomi's example that I love the most is that she was not a doormat. She didn't just remain mute when it came to her feelings or opinions. She kindly spoke her mind to her daughters-in-law and made her wishes clear. But, she knew when to be quiet.

The temptation for mothers-in-law is to go too far in one direction or the other. We either believe that our role is to just smile and not speak in order to keep the peace with our daughter-in-law or we talk too much spouting our wants and words of wisdom. Naomi knew how to hit the happy medium. She told her daughters-in-law more than once that they should go back to their people. Ruth 1:15 records the interaction. "'Look,' said Naomi, 'your sister-in-law is going back to her people and her gods. Go back with her.'" And then verse 18 says, "When Naomi realized that Ruth was determined to go with her, *she stopped urging her.*" (emphasis added) She knew it was time to be still.

We mothers-in-law need the discernment of Naomi so that we can know when to be quiet. That does not mean that we never voice an opinion, but we need to be sensitive and careful when our words are best left unsaid. When we do speak out of turn and say something that we shouldn't, our apology should come just as quickly as our misguided words did. "Oh God, help us to have Naomi's kind of wisdom."

The best thing my mother-in-law did for me was have my husband and give him life! She is such a giver, and will do anything to help us out.
—*Anonymous*

Do You Want to Be Right or Happy?

I distributed a survey about mothers-in-law to women throughout the country in every age category. It asked three questions: What is the best thing that your mother-in-law ever did for you? [past] What is the one thing that she does that drives you over the edge? [present] What one thing could she do to improve your relationship? [future] I will refer to the survey and the responses again, but for now, one thing that came through loud and clear is that we mothers-in-law can nag, coerce, and manipulate until we get what we want or until we prove that we are right. What is really happening is that we are systematically tearing down the relationship we have with our daughters-in-law. Dr. Phil, American television personality, author, and former psychologist has said on more than one occasion, "Do you want to be right or do you want to be happy?" Some of us pick "we want to be right no matter the cost."

Based on everything that Naomi knew, the totality of her life experiences, the culture in which she lived, she was giving "good" advice when she encouraged the girls to return to their homeland. She was, in essence, right. But, when she saw that Ruth was determined, "she stopped urging her." I know. That's easier said than done.

What difference does it make if we are right yet have no real relationship with someone that we are going to be attached to for the rest of our lives? We may know what is best because of age and experience, but when we continue to harp and push our way or our agenda we are really saying, "I don't trust you to make the right decisions." Our daughters-in-law are very astute at picking up our attitudes.

One young mother that responded to the previously mentioned survey had this very experience with her mother-in-law. Her response to the question, "What one thing does your mother-in-law do that drives you over the edge?" was telling. She wrote of herself that she is "not very strict about much, but I am very strict about [feeding my infant table food]. My baby is to be only breast fed and I make no exceptions until I am ready for them to eat something more. Because I have such terrible allergies, I am very paranoid about [my children] having them as well so I do everything I can to prevent it. Not only does she try to sneak and [feed them table food], but when I catch her and mention it, she is very disrespectful in her responses to me."

Her mother-in-law may be right according to her own life experiences. She probably had no difficulty with her own babies adjusting to table food and perhaps the table food would not have hurt her grandchildren either. However, that is not the point. This daughter-in-law felt belittled and disrespected when her mother-in-law disregarded her request. She felt as though she was not being "heard" because her mother-in-law discounted her request. Finally, she felt as though she was incompetent and not being trusted to raise her baby properly. Is that the message that you want to give your daughter-in-law? Do you want to engender in your daughter-in-law a feeling of insecurity or one of confidence? You have some choices to make here, mothers-in-law. Pray and ask the Holy Spirit to show you ways that you may be making your daughter-in-law feel torn down rather than built up. And, if you are really brave, ask her to point out to you the issues about which you nag.

The best thing my mother-in-law ever did for me was give me her son and a great potato peeler.
—*Anonymous*

Lessons Learned

Following is a summary of what we learned from Naomi as a mother-in-law:

- Naomi's selflessness enabled her to set her daughters-in-law free.
- She loved them despite the fact that they probably wouldn't have been her idea of the perfect daughters-in-law.
- She consistently acknowledged God's sovereign control over all of the circumstances of her life, even the difficult ones, and communicated this to her daughters-in-law.
- She knew when to give her opinion and when to remain quiet.

- She must have loved those girls unconditionally because of the complete devotion that she engendered from them.

Women continue to struggle with the same issues today that Naomi did centuries ago. What part of Naomi's story resonates with you? Perhaps you may be having difficulty setting your son and daughter-in-law free? Or you can relate only too well with the fact that Orpah and Ruth were possibly not Naomi's first choice as daughters-in-law. It could be the need to know when to speak and when to keep silent. Whichever one it is, you have to decide what you are going to do about it. That's what the rest of this book is about.

The best thing my mother-in-law ever did for me was raise a son that honors women.
—*Anonymous*

Chapter 2

Practical Preparation for Becoming a Mother-in-law

> "Direct your children onto the right path, and
> when they are older, they will not leave it."
> (Proverbs 22:6 NLT)

If I have caught you before the ring is on her finger, then this chapter is for you because being a good mother-in-law begins long before your children are of marriageable age. Just as we begin from our child's earliest days instilling ideals, morals and principles that we want them to have for a lifetime, we also begin instructing them about our values concerning a life mate. This is done both actively and passively. We teach them whether we are intentional in our training or not. We model what a marriage looks like. We model how a family communicates, settles disagreements, loves, laughs, and treats those outside of our immediate circle. We show them how a family earns and spends money. We demonstrate how we express our faith, how we pray, how we choose a church or whether we will attend church at all. We even model the relationship of a daughter-in-law and her mother-in-law. Through our interaction with our mother-in-law, we demonstrate a relationship that is loving and kind or one that is filled with contention and hard feelings. All of this is being observed by our children, even the things we try to hide, and it is forming their paradigm of family life. This representation from our family model becomes part of the equation in our child's choice of a spouse. Have you ever had the eerie feeling that you were being watched? You are!

This kind of teaching is passive because most of the time we are just living life and are not consciously aware of our children taking in our every move. We need to be aware, however, and intentional in how we interact as a family. Just as we are careful with our language and refrain from saying certain slang words in our children's presence because we don't want them repeating those words, we must show the same caution with our behavior and attitudes toward our spouse, in-laws and others.

I witnessed this being played out in my own extended family and didn't even realize until years later what a gift I had been given. As I referred to in the previous chapter, the mothers of my daughters-in-law did me the biggest favor they ever could have done by having great relationships with their own mothers-in-law. My daughters-in-law observed that interaction and went into their marriages thinking that was how things were supposed to be. They assumed that we would be friends, have fun together and enjoy one another's company. I don't believe it ever occurred to my girls' mothers that they were establishing a positive pattern that was going to be emulated into the next generation. They just lived their lives with integrity before their daughters. That modeling is a gift I treasure.

Whether we have sons or daughters, we want to do everything in our power to model the very best behavior in front of them. And, maybe as a bonus, we will give our children's future mothers-in-law the gift I was given. Within this chapter we will look at a biblical example of someone who exemplified the wonderful qualities that we want to possess.

I am blessed with a Godly mother-in-law whose company I truly enjoy! She is a wonderful example of what it means to serve others. She does so without complaining. Throughout the years, I've watched her agree to watch kids, bake goods for functions, support friends in going to home parties, pick up kids from school, shuttle people to doctor's offices and care for her ailing father, all tirelessly and without complaint. She has motivated me to serve in that same capacity. When I feel too tired or bothered to say yes to a friend who needs help with watching her kids, I remember my mother-in-law who would do anything and with a smile on her face.
—*Anonymous*

Spouse Specs

How do we teach our sons what to look for in a future wife? There is a short passage of Bible verses in Deuteronomy that perfectly illustrates how we are to live and instruct our children. "Love the LORD your God with all your heart and with all your soul and with all your strength. These commandments that I give you today are to be upon your hearts. Impress them on your children. Talk about them when you sit at home and when you walk along the road, when you lie down and when you get up. Tie them as symbols on your hands and bind them on your foreheads. Write them on the doorframes of your houses and on your gates." Deuteronomy 6:5-9

Do you see how instruction and teaching in Deuteronomy took place in the mundane happenings of life? We are to look for opportunities to coach and train our children while we are carrying on with the routine of our daily lives. Teaching moments concerning marriage or future spouses happen at unexpected times, perhaps when the subject of marriage comes up or when our children hear of a failed marriage. They can even happen when you are doing something as ordinary as tucking them into their beds at night. These are perfect times to talk about qualities to look for in a spouse.

What qualities should we be telling our young sons to look for? Many people familiar with the Bible might jump right to Proverbs 31 and whip out the list of things that woman was so proficient at doing and being. To tell you the truth, I can't even relate to the Proverbs 31 woman. She was too perfect and she set the standard so high that it seemed unattainable when I was a young wife. Even now it seems like a huge load to put on a future daughter-in-law.

When I revisit the book of Ruth, however, I find a woman who possessed wonderful qualities, but also knew suffering, loss, disappointment and failure. After all, she didn't have a baby the whole time that she was married to Naomi's son. She is someone who seems real, yet she provides an ideal pattern of qualities that any mother-in-law would love to have in a daughter-in-law and any daughter-in-law would love their mother-in-law to possess.

The emphasis in this section is to look at the qualities of Ruth in order to take a closer look at ourselves. We can and will be a pattern for our sons of the behavior traits he will look for in his future wife. The reality is that he will look at us first to see what qualities we exhibit. It matters very little what we tell our sons to look for in a girl if we are doing the opposite. Actions always drown out words. It makes sense that if my daughters-in-law could learn how to have a good relationship with me by watching their mothers interact with their mothers-in-law, then my sons could learn how to pick a wife by the character qualities that I live in front of them. I am shaping their view of what a wife is and how a wife acts. As we look at Ruth, take a look at yourself and see how you measure up to the virtues that you want your son to have in a wife. The best way to be a good mother-in-law is to be a person of character. That, in turn, paves the way for your son as he looks for his life choice in a mate.

1. **Ruth put her trust in Naomi's God.**

The factor of utmost importance to me was also the first thing I saw as I reread the book of Ruth, chapter 1, verse 16. It says, "But Ruth replied, 'Don't urge me to leave you or to turn back from you. Where you go I will go, and where you stay I will stay. Your people will be my people *and your God my God.*'" (emphasis added) Ruth recognized the true God and was willing to bank her entire future on Naomi and Naomi's God. She went on to say in verse 17, "Where you die I will die, and there I will be buried. May the *LORD* deal with me, be it ever so severely, if anything but death separates you and me." The word that Ruth used to describe Naomi's God was LORD. The original Hebrew for the word LORD is YHWH or Yahweh or Jehovah. The words refer to the "I AM," the only true God. In making that statement of total commitment to Naomi, she was actually showing a total commitment and trust in Naomi's God, the only true God. What an incredible influence Naomi had on Ruth! Naomi's relationship with God was so real and compelling that Ruth was willing to give up everything to belong to Naomi's God! Wouldn't we love to have that kind of positive influence on our daughters-in-law? We can if we have an authentic relationship with God.

Have you genuinely entrusted your life to Jesus? I'm not referring to associating with a certain religion or going to church, to being good or trying to do the right things. I am talking about telling God that you are done trying to run your own life because frankly, you haven't been very good at it. Have you placed your trust in the One who came to this earth and lived, was crucified, died, was buried, and then resurrected? Jesus came to restore all things and make them new again. Because of God's work on the cross through Jesus Christ, we can be made right with God and therefore, we can be made right with other people. When we place our trust in Him, God's Spirit begins a transformation in us to change us into His likeness. Christ has victory over all evil and brokenness. This sacrificial act changed everything. We now have hope for our future and we have hope for our relationships.

Death couldn't keep a sovereign God in the grave. As Paul indicates in his letter to the Romans, Christ's resurrection promises new life for us and in this action He calls each of us into a right relationship with God and right relationships with those who are in our lives. When we realize this and put our trust in Him instead of ourselves, we have entered into a new bond with Him. We are truly one of His children and are now identifying with the same LORD with whom Ruth identified. We have genuine faith. Once we have tasted the goodness of God, we want everyone to experience the same joy and peace, especially our sons and their future families.

As you are teaching your children the importance of being fully devoted to the LORD, the only true God, you can also impress upon them the worth of finding a spouse who shares that priority. Shared faith is so foundational to any marriage that if that doesn't exist, the couple begins their marriage on shaky ground. God said in His word, "If a house is divided against itself, that house cannot stand." (Mark 3:25) You thought that was Abraham Lincoln that said that? He got it from the book of Mark and Mark got it from Jesus. God really wants us to get this message, so He had it repeated in each of the first three gospels of the New Testament. It is critical that a couple have a shared faith and as Christians, it is critical that Christ be the basis of that faith.

2. Ruth had a good work ethic.

(Ruth 2:5-7), "Boaz asked the foreman of his harvesters, 'Whose young woman is that?' The foreman replied, 'She is the Moabitess who came back from Moab with Naomi. She said, 'Please let me glean and gather among the sheaves behind the harvesters.' 'She went into the field and *has worked steadily from morning till now*, except for a short rest in the shelter.'" (Emphasis added) Ruth was not afraid of a hard day's work. Her labors were pleasing to God because He values work.

In his book, *A Long Obedience in the Same Direction*, Eugene Peterson discusses God's view of work. "The Bible begins with the announcement, 'In the beginning God created', not 'sat majestic in the heavens,' and not 'was filled with beauty and love.' He created. He did something. He made something. He fashioned heaven and earth. The week of creation was a week of work. Genesis 1 is a journal of work. We live in a universe and in a history where God is working. Before anything else, work is an activity of God."

We can teach our sons that work is a gift from God to provide for ourselves and to be able to give to others. There is reward in work when see what our efforts have accomplished. Our children will develop their view of an honest day's work by what they see us doing. If we have a good work ethic, it will be the most natural thing for our sons to value that and look for a wife that demonstrates that same quality. He can begin discerning this by watching to see if she pitches in with household tasks at her home. Does she offer to help when she is at your house? Does she have a job? Or, is her attitude one of entitlement, laziness or that of a prima donna?

This is no guarantee that the girl your son falls in love with will have a great work ethic. The chances become much higher, however, when it is the only life that your son knows. It can only be that if it is the overriding atmosphere of your family to be hard workers.

3. Ruth had a humble spirit.

(Ruth 2:10), "At this, she bowed down with her face to the ground. She exclaimed, 'Why have I found such favor in your eyes that you notice me – a foreigner?'" Ruth was marked by humility. Her attitude was not arrogant or prideful. She was modest and respectful and did not consider herself better than any task or any person.

My pastor has a saying that convicts me to my toes every time I hear it. "You will know that you have a servant's heart by how you respond when you are treated like one." Oh my goodness! Why do I buck and rear against humility, against counting others better than myself, against serving, against putting myself out, against being completely at God's disposal? Because at the heart of every human being is self who longs to be God instead of allowing God to be God. True humility is being completely and utterly dependent upon our holy God.

Andrew Murray in his book entitled, *Humility* states, "Humility is the only soil in which the graces root; the *lack* of humility is the sufficient explanation of every defect and failure. Humility is not so much a grace or virtue along with others as it is the *root of all*, because it alone takes the right attitude before God and allows Him as God to do all."

An acquaintance of mine brazenly shared with me that in her household, "If Mamma ain't happy, ain't nobody happy." She smiled at me in a way that let me know she wasn't kidding. She wanted and even demanded that she be god in her home. Her world revolved around her to the detriment of her husband and children. No humble spirit found there. A few years later her family was torn apart by her affair with a co-worker. That affair didn't last and the story ended with "nobody happy."

A life lived in true humility is compelling because it is opposite of how our selfish world works. Recently, I landed on the TV show, Toddlers and Tiaras, and was stunned to hear a 5 year old say, "I'm spoiled. Being spoiled is getting what you want and no one else does." She is being systematically enabled to live a self-centered, winner-take-all lifestyle. Can you imagine what she will be like as a wife or daughter-in-law? Another mother of a three year old said, "I really do know that I am creating a monster." Oh my goodness! What are they doing? How will these little girls ever have successful marriages?

Humility is becoming more countercultural in our society with each passing day. However, when you demonstrate humility to your son by your lifestyle, it will be difficult for him to settle for anything less in his wife, which would be the opposite of these young ladies with an "all about me" attitude. Their mothers need to be arrested for child abuse. Does your son's girlfriend have a humble spirit? Do you?

4. Ruth had a sense of "other"ness.

"Other"ness describes a person whose radar is set to hone in on the needs, wants and wishes of other people out of love and concern for them. It puts others above oneself. It shows genuine interest in the other person.

Ruth had a sense of selflessness that was displayed in her loyalty toward and care of Naomi. It was so remarkable that people took notice and told others about it. "Boaz replied, 'I've been told all about *what you have done for your mother-in-law since the death of your husband....*'" (Ruth 2:11a). (emphasis added)

I have been going to lunch with a friend once a month for years so that we can catch up on each other's lives and families and be accountable to one another. During one of those lunch dates I discovered that my friend not only had been listening to what I shared, but she had my prayer concerns typed into her phone so that she could pray for me and my requests at certain times. She showed real concern and care for me by listening, writing down my prayer requests and then praying for me. Who wouldn't love a friend like that?

Do you want to check your "other"ness gauge? Go to lunch with someone and keep mental notes of how much you talk about yourself and how many times you ask her about her life or her interests. If you really want to know how "other" inclined you are, go and determine that the whole visiting time is going to be about her. That exercise will reveal how other-focused or self-focused you are.

Your children will discern from a young age if you are a person who cares for and invests in other people. When a person is genuinely "other" focused, not only your children, but the world will take notice. It is much more likely that your son will choose a wife that cares for others if he has had that quality modeled in his home.

Teach your son to be on the lookout for demonstrations of "other"ness as he considers whom to date. He should look for a girl who is kind and cares about those who are marginalized or suffering. Is she thoughtful, considerate, sympathetic, or compassionate? Or course, no one is going to possess all of these qualities all of the time, but if the girl your son is interested in shows little of any of these traits, tell him to *run*!

5. Ruth had a Good Reputation

Again, I will quote Ruth 2:11a, "Boaz replied, *'I've been told* all about what you have done for your mother-in-law since the death of your husband...'" (emphasis added) The first part of verse 11 clearly illustrates Ruth's stellar reputation that preceded her into Judah. The tender way in which she cared for her mother-in-law was as countercultural in that day and age as it is today. It was so incredible that it caused a buzz of gossip among the Israelites. The news reached Boaz before Ruth did. A woman with character like that was welcomed into his fields to glean. It's not difficult to imagine that a woman with that kind of reputation and character would be welcomed into your family as well.

There is much to say, both positively and negatively about relying on someone having a good reputation. It is true that you can't believe everything that people say. It is also true that you shouldn't listen to gossip. I even concede that God can change and completely transform anyone's life. Those are all important things to teach your son. But, it is equally important to emphasize to him that if *many* people whom he deeply respects tell him something or warn him about someone, *he should listen.* This concept needs to be learned before our son falls head over heels for a girl and is blinded by his love.

6. Ruth Displayed an Attitude of Gratitude

As we continue reading the conversation between Ruth and Boaz we read the following, "'May I continue to find favor in your eyes, my lord,' she said. 'You have given me comfort and have spoken kindly to your servant...'" (Ruth 2:13a) All of Boaz' kindnesses did not go unnoticed by Ruth. She didn't take anything for granted and was grateful for everything he had done for her including the way he spoke to her. She didn't just stop at feeling grateful, but she spoke her gratitude.

One of the first things that impressed me most about our daughter-in-law, Nicole, while she and our son, Matt, were dating, was that she always freely expressed gratitude. Every time she ate with us, she would thank me for the good meal. If I bought her something or if she visited our home, we would promptly receive a thank you note. They have now been married almost six years and her attitude of gratitude with us is incredible. Her Mom and Dad should be very proud that their daughter listened carefully to that life lesson that they taught her.

Teach your son to have a grateful spirit and then train him to look for a wife with that same attitude. The lessons begin by watching you as he grows. Do you say "thank you" to the members of your family when they do even small things around your home? Do you make it a habit of showing gratitude to your husband and children for gifts or kind actions? Do you write thank you notes? Teaching your son to look for a wife that will show gratitude begins with you demonstrating the importance of a grateful spirit day in and day out.

7. Ruth was Generous

(Ruth 2:18), "She carried it [the barley] back to town, and her mother-in-law saw how much she had gathered. Ruth also brought out and gave her what she had left over after she had eaten enough." If anyone was entitled to eat every morsel of the food given her, it was Ruth. She had worked a long, hot, back-breaking day in the barley fields. Then she carried a half bushel of barley, which weighs approximately 24 pounds, home to Naomi. On top of all of that, she gave Naomi the leftovers from her lunch. Now that is generous.

Recently, my husband and I had the privilege of hearing a sermon series on generosity. The emphasis was on using our time, talents and treasures for God and His purposes. At the end of each sermon, our pastor encouraged us to pray and ask God what He would have us do that week to express generosity to others because of how generous God has been to us.

The Sunday that he preached on being generous with our talents a friend of ours said that he prayed and knew instantly what he was to do that week. Luke is a woodworking teacher at a high school in our area. He and his wife had planned a two-day get away before school started, had their child care arranged and were set to go. But, they couldn't decide where to go and were still debating until that very Sunday when God decided what they would be doing and where they would be going. They have dear friends who are seminary students with three children. In other words, they are not well off. Their bathroom had been in disrepair for two years. This young couple had moved into a house they could afford thinking that they would get the destroyed drywall in their bathroom fixed when they had enough money. They would save money to repair it and then the money would be needed for some other thing. This particular weekend they were gone and Luke just happened to know where the key to their home was. Luke told his wife, Shannon what he had been thinking and she said, "OK. But we are on a budget and we must stick to the budget!" She admitted that she is not a great giver. As they totally gutted their friend's bathroom and began purchasing light fixtures, faucets and drywall, she found God changing her attitude. She said, "We tripled our budget and it did not taste bitter at all. It was fun. Now I am bitten by the generosity bug!" Their friends were overcome when they got home and went in to find a newly remodeled bathroom. They cried when they shared with the congregation how blessed they were to receive such a lavish gift from friends. They were so grateful to Luke and Shannon and to God for prompting Luke to use his talents to bless them. Luke and Shannon were overwhelmed with gratefulness to God that they could be a part of bringing good to their friends. It was a circle of blessing.

That is what God does. He gives us the resources to share with others and when we do, it causes our hearts to rejoice and turn to Him with gratitude. "This service that you perform is not only supplying the needs of the Lord's people but is also *overflowing in many expressions of thanks to God. Because of the service by which you have proved yourselves, others will praise God* for the obedience that accompanies your confession of the gospel of Christ, and for your generosity in sharing with them and with everyone else." (2 Corinthians 9:12-13) (emphasis added) When we are generous, we let go of our "stuff" to hang onto God.

Do your sons see you habitually exhibit a generous spirit? Do they see you take a meal to someone who is sick or who has just had a baby? Do they find extra children in your home when they get back from school, as you help out a young mother? Do they know that you give money to missionaries, disaster relief or to a family that can't pay a bill this month? Is the atmosphere of your home one of generosity?

Teach your son to look for the quality of generosity in his friends and potential girlfriends. You can tell him to observe if she hoards things or holds loosely to her possessions. Does she give to the needy? Does she give to her church? Generosity is definitely a quality that your son will want in a wife.

8. Ruth was Wise and Could Take Advice.

After Ruth reported to Naomi the happenings of the day, Naomi gave her very good advice. (Ruth 2:22-23a), "Naomi said to Ruth her daughter-in-law, 'It will be good for you, my daughter, to go with his girls, because in someone else's field you might be harmed.' So Ruth stayed close to the servant girls of Boaz to glean until the barley and wheat harvests were finished...."

Have you noticed that there are some people that won't listen to anyone? If they are given counsel, they dig in and do the opposite. Those types of people always have to learn the hard way. I sure hope that you are not one of them.

Ruth was willing to listen and cooperate with the guidance of her mother-in-law. She recognized that in this situation her mother-in-law knew what was best and Ruth was sensible enough to follow Naomi's advice. It takes wisdom and maturity to heed good advice. Are you modeling those before your family? Are you willing to listen to the advice of others who are wiser than you? Being able to take advice and having wisdom go hand in hand and are two additional qualities that we can teach our boys to have and to look for in a future spouse.

9. Ruth had Noble Character.

(Ruth 3:11b), "...All my fellow townsmen know that you are a woman of noble character."

The sum of all of the traits embodied in Ruth and listed above is character. Character has been defined by H. Jackson Brown, Jr., author of *Life's Little Instruction Book*, as "what we do when we think no one is looking." Ruth had no idea that generations upon generations of people would be looking at her life. Yet, we have found her to be an incredible role model of what we would like to be and what we would want for our sons to have in a wife.

There is no perfect person. We haven't been perfect mothers, we won't be perfect mothers-in-law and there will not be a perfect daughter-in-law. All of us are flawed by our humanity and sin. Ruth was not perfect and without sin, and your daughter-in-law won't be either. Mothers-in-law, we need to remember that even if our sons fall in love with the "right" girl, she is still young and although she may be very wise, she has not had the life experiences that we have had. We need to be lavish in giving grace. When he does find "that" girl, don't be surprised and don't panic if she is someone who is his total opposite in temperament and personality. He may even fall in love with someone who is totally different from you. (Heaven forbid!) God will use those very differences to refine all of you to be more like Christ. What we have seen in Ruth and what we want to live out in front of our sons and teach our sons to look for goes deeper than personality or temperament; it goes to character. We can instruct our sons to be men of character and look for a woman of character who demonstrates the "spouse specs" that Ruth had: love God first, have a good work ethic, be a person of humility, have a good reputation, possess a sense of otherness, an attitude of gratitude, a generous spirit, be able to take advice, be wise and finally be a person of character. But, it starts with us. We need to be those things before our son can even begin to look for a wife with those same qualities. Pick just one of the character traits that Ruth possessed and begin being more diligent in developing that in your life. Your home will change and so will your son's perspective. Who needs the Proverbs 31 woman? We have Ruth! Oh. Maybe Ruth *is* a Proverbs 31 woman.

The best thing my mother-in-law ever did for me was while I was pregnant and on bed rest, she came to my house every day and waited on me hand and foot. [She] did all of my laundry, cooked and cleaned!
—*Anonymous*

Model Mother

This is not a book on child rearing. There are many wonderful people who know a lot more about that than I do. But, may I share one quick thought on the subject that will be of help? Long before you become a mother-in-law you are a mother. You want to live the kind of life that will cause your son to care about and value your opinions as to whom he dates and whom he will marry. Live with such integrity that he will genuinely respect what you think about his girlfriend. Conduct yourself with such wisdom that if you voice a concern about her he will be willing to consider and seriously weigh what you have to say. It all starts when he is young. The foundation on which he builds his trust in you and your opinion leads to having a good relationship with your son. Love him unconditionally. Be his biggest encourager and cheerleader. Don't try to live your hopes and dreams through him. Don't baby him, pick at him or set unreal expectations of him. "Do not provoke your children to anger by the way you treat them. Rather bring them up with discipline and instruction that comes from the Lord." (Ephesians 6:4 NLT) If you raise your son according to the standard set in God's word with love and discipline and instruction, it is much more likely he will want his parent's input and approval on the woman he's considering marrying.

The best thing that my mother-in-law ever did for me was when we got married, she LET HIM GO! She told us that she will not be meddlesome, or overbearing, and that she did the best she could raising him, and understood it was time to let him live his life with his new wife and family.
—Anonymous

Pray for Your Son's Future Wife

Almost every little boy at some point in his life looks up at his mommy lovingly and says, "Mommy, when I grow up, I want to marry you." When our boys said that to me I replied, "Sorry, I'm already married to Daddy." There would usually be a response similar to, "Well I'll just marry you too." They didn't quite get the concept. I'm sure that you have had an experience very similar to that with your son. Moments like that offer the perfect opportunity to let your son know that you are praying for his future wife. Tell him that if it is in God's plan for him to marry, you are praying that at the perfect time God will bring the right girl into his life. Let him know that your prayer is that he will have a deep assurance that she is the one that you have been praying for all of this time.

It may seem strange to pray for your future daughter-in-law, but it becomes a huge blessing. If you don't know how you can pray for someone that you have never met nor even put a face on, here's a tip. Tailor your prayers for her according to how old your son is and what is going on in his life. If he has a test at school that day, is having difficulty in a particular subject or is struggling with a friendship, use those things in your prayers for your "daughter-in-law to be." An example would be, "Father, You know exactly who she is and You see what is happening in her life today. Only You know if she is suffering or stressing about a test. Make her aware of Your presence. Help her to run to You as her security and source of strength." Pray the same things for her that you long to have happen in the life of your son. Ask God to guide you by His Spirit in your prayers for your future daughter-in-law. You'll be surprised what comes to your mind as you pray that you never would have thought about on your own.

Let your son know that you are praying for his future wife. It shows him the value that you put on this life decision. Your prayers illustrate to your son the care and concern you have for him and the investment that you are continually making in his life.

The best thing my mother-in-law ever did for me was check on me and let me know that she was there for me to talk to during a time when I was really depressed and my husband was out of the country.
—Anonymous

Deal Breakers

Deal Breakers can vary according to your family's culture, value system and tolerance level. The important thing is to figure out with your son ahead of time what would be a real deal breaker for all of you.

How one handles conflict or money or whether one is a slob or neat freak do not have to be deal breakers. Those are the types of things that can be worked on or worked out in premarital counseling. We have already discussed that no one is perfect so there are some things that you just have to decide to live with. Only your son can decide what those things are. Ask him this question as a barometer of his tolerance level with a particular flaw that bothers him, "Is _____ something that you can live with for the rest of your life?"

There are some things that are more than red flags. They are checkered flags, as in take off in the opposite direction. I am not a marriage counselor, but I know some warning signs. The first deal breaker in my book is if the couple doesn't share the same faith in Christ. We have already talked about that being the foundation to a successful Christian marriage. Pray and then instruct your son to give serious attention to God's word when it says, "Do not be yoked [or tethered] with unbelievers. For what do righteousness and wickedness have in common or what fellowship can light have with darkness?" (2 Cor. 6:14) There are worse things than never marrying. One of those things is to be in a miserable relationship in which the two cannot even share their most important beliefs.

The other major deal breaker is if there is a severe character flaw (narcissism, habitual lying, cheating, patterns of laziness, addiction to gambling, pornography or any other sexual addictions that have not been seriously dealt with). There are some character flaws that, short of an absolute miracle from God, will never change even after years of counseling. Marrying someone with a gigantic character flaw will lead to a lifetime of heartache. *Please warn your children that believing they can change someone is a recipe for disaster!*

What I am about to say is controversial in Christian circles, but I believe that I need to share it. I used to tell our boys when they were small that the most important thing they should look for in a girlfriend or wife is that she is a follower of Jesus. That's true, but one can love Jesus and still have deep-seated emotional problems that can deter them from having a meaningful, thriving, growing, giving relationship. It's not impossible to be married to someone with these kinds of emotional issues. Nothing is impossible with God. But life is much more enjoyable and productive if one's spouse is mentally and emotionally healthy and doesn't exhibit any of the character flaws mentioned above.

There is no perfect girl so don't lead your sons to believe that. All of us have something with which to deal. I am not referring to the run-of-the-mill emotional ups and downs of life. I *am* talking about severe emotional problems and personality defects. God is in the business of redemption and can turn around any bad situation. Marrying a person with drastic emotional problems can work, but it also may be a life of sheer misery. Your son's marriage has a much better opportunity to be successful if he falls in love with an emotionally stable girl.

There are other red flags that don't have to totally kill the deal, but they need to be seriously considered before a marriage takes place. Are there step-children involved? Is there an overbearing extended family member that won't let go? Is the person that your son is serious about someone who has difficulty handling money? Is that person self-centered? Is she one who is persistently indecisive? Is he a little bit country and she is a little bit rock and roll? OK. That was an obscure song reference, but hopefully you are tracking where I am going.

I can't tell you what your deal breaker should be, but I can suggest that you think it through and talk about it with your son. He needs to have his mind made up before he meets that cute little girl that he wants to rescue.

My mother-in-law has a heart of <u>gold!</u> There is nothing she wouldn't do for me or her entire family. I thank God I have her in my life. On our wedding day, she lovingly gave me two gifts. The first was her mother's locket and the second was a recipe for my husband's favorite meal. Tamale pie! Both gifts mean the world to me!!
—*Anonymous*

No Guilt

If you are reading this book, there is a good chance that your son is already engaged or married (unless you are proof-reading it, young bride, before you give it to your new mother-in-law!) You may be saying to yourself, "Oh great. It's too late. I didn't do any of those things. I didn't pray for my son's future wife. I didn't even think to talk to him about qualities that would be good in a wife. No wonder things are rough with my daughter-in-law!" Let yourself off of the hook. Really. We can't do anything about the past but confess it then move on. My mother has said to me many times that she prays that God will heal every mistake and dumb thing that she ever did while raising me. You can do that too. Don't give into temptation to keep going back to something that you can't change. Ask God to redeem it and turn every mistake that you made into something that will bring good to your son and his family and glory to God. Begin right now to do what you can and go away from reading this guilt free!

The best thing my mother-in-law has done for me is that she has allowed my family to live in her home for 19 months and has never asked us when we are moving out.
—Anonymous

Chapter 3

He's Engaged!

> "My son, if your heart is wise, then my
> heart will be glad indeed."
> (Proverbs 23:15)

Make the Decision to Love Her

The ring is now on her finger and in the best case scenario you love her almost as much as your son does. However, things don't always work out "best case scenario." Despite how you view their relationship at this moment, you, future mother-in-law, have an opportunity right from the beginning of your son's engagement to set the relationship between you and your new daughter-in-law on the right course. Your actions and attitudes now can make all of the difference for the entire rest of your years as mother-in-law to this dear girl. Perhaps you are elated at your son's choice and are convinced that he married up. Many of you may not know what to feel because you simply don't know her very well. Then there is the group of you future mothers-in-law that are seriously considering hari-kari because you were hoping he would pick anyone but her.

I found this simple prayer in the margin of my mother-in-law's Bible study book. "Lord, my voice is weak so I can no longer teach, but I can encourage others through cards and letters." Her ministry in this was far-reaching. What a wonderful lesson that God will always provide ways that we can serve others if we are yielded to His will.
—Anonymous

Oh No! Not Her!

If you find yourself in the latter group, keep praying. It is not a done deal until they say "I do." Have a frank conversation with your son and tell him of your concerns and why you have the apprehension that you do. Ask him to prayerfully consider your thoughts. It is likely that if you tell him straight out to *dump that girl*, he will become defensive and will do the opposite. Nobody his age wants to be bossed around by his mother. If you approach your son with humility and show genuine love and concern for both him and his fiancée, he will be much more likely to consider what you have to say. Tell him that you are praying for both of them to make the right decision and then pray. In the meantime, be kind and loving to his fiancée. That is how true believers in Jesus Christ act. If you look down on her or treat her shabbily, your son will feel protective of her and your actions will push them closer together.

I know of a mother and grandmother of a young man who were completely distraught over his choice of a bride. They saw disturbing qualities in his fiancée and felt sure that the marriage would be doomed from the start. Those two went to work praying fervently and earnestly. They were thrilled when the wedding was called off hours before it was to take place. Even the prospective groom seemed relieved.

There is always hope that God will intercede and that everyone will come to their senses. But, the outcome of your prayers may not be the same as that mom and grandma's. If God chooses to answer your prayers differently, you can be sure that He can bring good from the situation and that good might be the refining of your soul.

Finally, if you don't like her but you're not sure why, take a close look at yourself while you are asking him to reevaluate his engagement. Is it your problem? Would you consider anyone good enough for him? Are you simply afraid of losing him? Are you jealous?

My mother-in-law has written some sweet notes and cards to me that I appreciate.
—Anonymous

Choose Love

Regardless of how you feel about your son's choice in a wife, there are proactive steps that you can take to better your relationship with his new bride-to-be. The first thing to do is make the mental choice that you are going to love her. Dr. Gary Smalley has written a book called, *Love is a Decision*. In that book he teaches us that love is not an emotion or a warm, fuzzy feeling. Love is a verb, an action word. You can decide to love and then act on that decision, despite how you feel. With God's help you can love her without strings attached, without reservation, or without conditions. Who doesn't need someone in her life to love her like that? Your daughter-in-law needs to be loved even when she has acted immaturely, when she has said things that are unkind or thoughtless, when she has totally messed up. When we show love in the face of those kinds of behaviors, we are demonstrating the kind of love that Jesus has for us. That kind of unconditional love is drawing. It is irresistible. No one can continue to resist someone who loves them unconditionally. The choice is yours. What are you going to decide to do?

How can one love like that? It sounds good, even honorable but totally unattainable. Consider though, would God command us to do something that He isn't able to accomplish in us?

We begin by fixing our full attention and meditating on the mercy of God in our lives. When we look at the cross and what Christ did for us, we realize that He loves us with an unconditional love. "Very rarely will anyone die for a righteous man, though for a good man someone might possibly dare to die. But God demonstrates his own love for us in this: While we were still sinners, Christ died for us." (Romans 5:7-8). Despite the way we have treated God by ignoring Him, defying Him and even denying Him, He willingly gave up His life for us. He loved us knowing that He will get nothing from most of us in return. He can enable you to love others, even a daughter-in-law that gets on your last nerve, one who does not write thank you notes, a girl who never returns a call, one whose life is totally about her, or, you fill in the blank. Yes. God can help you love even that kind of person. Focus on His mercy to you. If you need something more tangible, make a list of the good things in your life. Get a piece of paper and write down every blessing. "Every good and perfect gift is from above, coming down from the Father of the heavenly lights, who does not change like shifting shadows." (James 1:17) Every good thing in your life is a result of God's mercy to you. Remember the love that you have been shown by God and then pray and ask God to help you show the same mercy to your daughter-in-law. Ask Him to give you His heart for this new girl in your life.

The next thing that you can do is reframe your thoughts concerning how you are to love her. Don't grit your teeth, squeak out a prayer and demonstrate a form of love that acts like, "OK. I'll look like I love her because I have to." If you are truly concentrating on God's mercy, I doubt if you will have that attitude. There is another verse that we can center our attention on in the book of Romans that will help us to see that loving our daughters-in-law is not just something we do for her or for our sons or even for us but for a God who loves us. It is: "Owe no one anything, except to love each other..." (Romans 13:8a) You love your daughter-in-law because it is the debt that you owe God for what He has done for you. The mortgage company does not call you every month and congratulate you for paying your bill. When you pay a debt, you are merely doing what is required of you. If you are a Jesus follower, you will love your daughter-in-law. It is the debt that you owe. God can help the emotion to come after the actions. If it never comes, however, you can still love because "love is a verb."

Loving someone unconditionally does not mean that it is going to be a relationship free of conflict or disagreements. Those types of relationships are reserved for Heaven. It does mean that you talk through the tension always with the underlying attitude of love and understanding. If she won't talk, then you talk to God.

It is important to let your future daughter-in-law know that you love her. Tell her even if you don't have the ooey-gooey feeling. If the blunt, "I love you," head-on approach is not your style, then tell her how blessed you feel that she is going to be part of your son's life and your family. (If indeed you do feel blessed and happy that she is going to share your last name. If you can't say that to her because you just don't feel that way, pray that you will. Emotion follows action.) Let her know that you have prayed for her and you can't wait to see how God works in her life and your son's life as they come together in marriage.

If you are thrilled with this lovely girl who is about to become your daughter-in-law, let her know. Besides the direct approach there is another way to communicate love to her. Contact her parents and tell them. I just had lunch with a dear friend whose son and new bride eloped one year ago. Both sets of parents were disappointed at the choice that this bride and groom made. My friend expressed to me that was not how she always dreamed things would be when her son got married. Everyone felt a little robbed because they didn't get to witness the sacred occasion. Feelings were raw for a while and things were stilted between the two sets of parents and between the parents and kids. Within the last year the situation has become much more congenial and my friend, who has always loved her daughter-in-law, has fallen even more in love with her. So here they are a year later planning a great wedding in which the bride and the groom will renew their vows in front of all of the family and friends that the parents did not get to invite this time last year.

My friend wants to express to the bride's family how much she loves their daughter and what a fine job they did in raising her so she is writing a letter to them to be read at the Rehearsal Dinner expressing her feelings. Can you imagine how affirming that will be to the bride's family and to that young bride? Telling her parents how much you love their daughter will be a source of encouragement to them and to your wonderful new daughter-in-law.

Another thing you can do is tell others in her hearing how much you love her. Overhearing you telling people how great you think she is makes her feel safe and secure in this new tenuous relationship with you. It reinforces to her that you are on her side and that you have no intention of being her adversary. Wouldn't hearing positive things like that from your mother-in-law have been comforting to you as you started off your marriage?

The best thing my mother-in-law ever did for me was share with me her passion for gardening.
—Anonymous

Getting to Know Your New Daughter-in-law

You have decided to love her, now you have their entire engagement to get to know her better. Depending upon your previous knowledge of her, there are things that you can do to really know this girl who will soon be the most important woman in your son's life.

Hopefully you have been having dialogue all along with your son about his girlfriend. If you have not yet done this, talk to your son about his fiancée. What attracted him to her? What great qualities does she have? What makes him believe that she is the one for him? This will give you a picture of how he sees her. Then, if circumstances and distance allow, spend as much time with her as possible. Go out to lunch, go shopping, have her visit your home. Do all of the things that you would do if you really wanted to know a friend better. Show genuine interest in her, her hobbies, her likes and dislikes. Keep in mind that she does not have to like the same things that you do. Ask her questions without interrogating her. Most people love to talk about themselves and tell their stories.

Be an observer of your "daughter-in-law-to-be." Don't be a stalker, but watch her and study how she gives and receives love. That is called her "love language." There is a wonderful book by Dr. Gary Chapman entitled, *The Five Languages of Love*. In that book he states that there are five main ways people give and receive love. Those methods of communicating love are demonstrated through having quality time together, personal touch, acts of service, giving and receiving gifts, and hearing words of affirmation. Misunderstandings can come between you and your daughter-in-law when she receives love in a completely different way than you are trying to convey it. If your daughter-in-law's love language is words of affirmation and yours is acts of service, you can be running yourself ragged trying to let her know how much you love her by all of the things that you are doing for her and your efforts are falling flat. You are probably getting frustrated because she just doesn't seem to appreciate it or respond to your efforts. The problem is not what you are doing but how you are trying to let her know that you love her. In a "words of affirmation" girl, you just need to tell her right out that you love her and think that she is the very best thing that ever happened to your son. If you cannot say that yet, compliment her on a certain quality that she has. That works wonders for someone whose love language is words of affirmation.

How can you discover your new daughter-in-law's love language? Watch her. What she does for people, particularly your son is probably how she best receives love. We most often express our love for others in the way that we best receive it. If she loves to give him gifts even if they are small, her love language is probably gifts. If she loves to help him whether he is working on his car or doing a big project for his job, her love language is very likely acts of service. Discern through observation and through discussions with your son what her love language is and then use it!

By making the decision to love your new daughter-in-law and communicating it in a way that she truly understands, you are smoothing the path to a great relationship. You are proving to her that although it may be conventional wisdom that a mother-in-law and daughter-in-law don't get along, that is not how it has to be for the two of you. Decide in your heart and mind that as much as it is up to you, you are going to live at peace and in harmony with her and you are going to be her greatest cheerleader. If none of the above is motivation enough, remember, she will most likely be the one that holds the keys to you seeing your grandchildren in the future!

The best thing my mother-in-law ever did for me was come to our home to serve our family after each baby was born. She helped with cooking and cleaning and taking care of the other children which allowed me to be alone with the baby!
—Anonymous

The "Should" List

Depending on the personality and temperament of your new daughter-in-law, there is a tool that you can use to set the groundwork for a good relationship with her. Encourage her to write a "Should List" of all of the things she thinks a mother-in-law "should" be or do. You do the same, writing *your* ideas of what a mother-in-law should be. At an appointed time, get together and show each other your lists and have a discussion about them. This opens up conversation and lets both of you begin your relationship with common expectations. If she is game and willing, you can do the same thing for what you both perceive the perfect daughter-in-law to be. One needs to be very careful at this point because your daughter-in-law-to-be is at a more inherently insecure stage of life right now. If both willingly agree, however, it gives each of you the chance to say how you can or cannot meet the other's expectations. Making the "Should List" is a proactive activity that can dispel misconceptions and wards off unmet expectations before they happen.

Before you even ask this of your new daughter-in-law, you really need to evaluate whether it would be a help or a hindrance. To many girls this will feel intimidating and daunting and would be counterproductive. Your willingness to take a look at yourself, your readiness to consider her age, maturity level, personality, and temperament, and the nature and quality of your relationship up until now all need to be taken into consideration before you dive into asking her to embark on this exercise. Remember the goal is to have a great relationship, not get the answers to your questions or make sure that you complete a list. If she loves a challenge and this is right up her alley, it can be a great tool to help you understand one another better.

This sounds corny but the best thing my mother-in-law has done for me is have my husband. He is so wonderful to me!
—Anonymous

Practice, Practice, Practice

The months of your son's engagement are usually packed with activity leading up to the wedding day. The bride and groom are busy with bridal showers, choosing invitations, selecting flowers and trying to book venues for the wedding and reception. But what should the mother of the groom be doing during this time? The engagement provides the perfect opportunity to practice; practice letting go, practice loving your new daughter-in-law and practice keeping your mouth closed. God gives you this time to get used to the idea that your son and his future wife are now adults. Hasn't it been your goal to raise a man all along? You have raised this boy to grow up and be a man and it is now time to unclench your fingers and allow him to do just that. If you practice during the engagement, it will be much easier to finally and officially release him on his wedding day. It is almost time to see how well you did.

The best thing that my mother-in-law ever did for me was create a room for me in which I could go "hide" when I went to visit their house. She and my father-in-law rearranged the bedrooms in their house, and moved a love seat into the upstairs guest bedroom. They also put an end table with a lamp on it, and a TV on the dresser. When we went to visit, she showed me the bedroom and said, "I know you enjoy reading, and I wanted you to have a place where you could comfortably read or watch TV." I felt like she knew me and acknowledged what I like and what I needed.
—*Anonymous*

Chapter 4

Keeping the Wedding from Becoming a Nightmare

> "Therefore, a man shall leave his father and mother and
> be joined to his wife, and they shall become one flesh."
> **(Genesis 2:24 NKJV)**

I went from loving this verse from the Bible when I was a young bride to being irritated by it when my son was preparing to marry. I thought it was brilliant when it was directed to my mother-in-law, but I didn't like it nearly as well when I became a mother-in-law. God might as well have said, "Do you *get this*?" The message that He is relaying to us is, "The moment the words 'I do' are said, your little boy's allegiance is no longer to you but to that young girl standing next to him." *She* is now the most important person in your son's life. You can argue or pout about it all you want, but it is God's plan and although it may not seem like it at the moment, His way is always the best way.

Mamas, one of the hard, cruel facts of life is that we ruined our figures having those boys, we invested all of that time, energy and money in them and what do they do? They dump us for another girl! But, it is absolutely biblical though perhaps hard to swallow. Don't put him in a position where he has to choose between you and his new bride. You will be going against a principle that was established in the very first book of the Bible and you may be setting yourself up for hurt, embarrassment and disappointment.

Remember when you were a young bride? You wanted your new husband's full loyalty and commitment. You wanted to be the one that he ran to first for comfort and advice. You didn't want him going to his mother before he came to you. You must give your daughter-in-law what you so badly wanted from your mother-in-law; respect, dignity and space.

Dear mothers-in-law, if we could really get this one point and accept it, we would have more peace within ourselves and within our extended family. Don't "kick against the goads." Do you recognize this New Testament Biblical reference? When Christ revealed Himself to the Apostle Paul on the road to Damascus he said to him, "Saul, Saul, why do you persecute me? It is hard for you to kick against the goads." (Acts 26:14) It was a common saying in the Jewish world and would have been easily understood for the readers of that time, but for us, not so much.

A goad was a long stick with a spike on the end that the farmers of that day used to control their livestock. Now don't go getting ideas. A stubborn animal would kick out against the spike doing harm to itself. The more that the willful beast rebelled, the more it suffered.

You're getting the picture, aren't you? Do you know that your daughter-in-law may be saying in her mind, to her friends, to your son or even on Facebook, "Why is she persecuting me? Why does she talk down to me? Why does she ignore or disregard everything that I say? Why does she treat me like I don't know anything?" If you haven't internalized and accepted the important fact that your son's allegiance is now hers, you are kicking against the goads and *you* will be the one who suffers the most. The other alternative is that you destroy their marriage when that girl is finally run off. That is *not* a good option.

How do mothers successfully step aside and let his allegiance turn to his new wife? How do we let go and come to terms with the fact that he now belongs to her? To some women it is intuitive. To others of us it comes with a little more work. There are two tools that are available to us that can be of tremendous help. In fact, we can begin by practicing the use of these tools during our son's engagement. If we use them throughout his marriage, we will be very successful mothers-in-law.

The first tool is to have a great memory. Come on mother-in-law! Don't you remember when you walked down the aisle and said "I do" to that handsome, young guy of yours? Do you remember how you wanted, even longed to be treated by your new mother-in-law? And even if she was loving and kind toward you, you did *not* want your husband going to her before you when an important decision was to be made or he was hurt and needed to talk or even when he needed a great meal. You wanted your dashing new husband to come to you, to prefer you over his mother and to pick you over her if there was a choice to be made.

Remember the kind of mother-in-law that you wanted to have. Remember what she did that made you feel loved (or not). Remember what your mother-in-law did that made you crazy. Remember. Think. Reflect. Even make lists for yourself and decide in your heart that with God's help you will try to be the kind of mother-in-law that you wanted.

Another thing to remember is that you raised your son and taught him the values that he now has. This man that you raised and trained and gave the very best years of your life has chosen *her*. He must see something of value in her. Trust your son and honor his choice. Trust that the life lessons that you poured into him stuck and he used much that you taught him to pick his new wife.

The second tool that you will need to use is prayer. I've had mothers-in-law say to me, "But what if my daughter-in-law is difficult? What if she is distant? What if she is dumb?" Ok, no one has said that last one, but they have implied it and I couldn't resist the alliteration. What if??? Pray. Ask God to help you remember what you were like when you were young. Ask Him to give you a love for your daughter-in-law that you can't drum up on your own. Ask Him to give you patience. Ask Him to glue your mouth shut. Pray that God will bless her and her relationship with your son. Pray that good will come their way. Most importantly, ask God to let you see your new daughter-in-law like He sees her and love her like He loves her. Pray. Pray. Pray.

Often what happens when we pray is that instead of God changing the circumstance, He changes us and our attitude. Have you ever had God move you from a hateful attitude toward someone to genuine love for them? I have, and love feels a lot better.

If you can't even make yourself formulate words to say to God on her behalf because the situation is so contentious or repugnant then purchase a book containing written prayers and read those putting her name in each appropriate place. Pray scripture for her. Ask God to transform the difficult circumstance or transform you. There is a wonderful book that I have used for praying scripture for years. It is made up of Bible verses organized into categories and is entitled, *Praying God's Will for Your Husband* by Lee Roberts. I also use this book to pray for my sons and my daughters-in-law by simply putting their names in each verse instead of my husband's. This would be the perfect tool to use to pray for your daughter-in-law. If you prefer, Lee Roberts has also written a book entitled, *Praying God's Will for Your Children* that you can also use to pray for your daughter-in-law.

What often happens in our culture isn't necessarily that there is bad blood between the mother-in-law and the new daughter-in-law, but that they simply don't know each other very well. It is likely that your son and his wife met in college or in the workplace and your encounters with her have been very intermittent or limited. Unfortunately, it is conventional wisdom that the mother-in-law/daughter-in-law relationship is predisposed to be negative. So you find yourself faced with a young gal that you hardly know and she likely comes to you wary of how she will be received and treated. The way you respond to her can change every preconceived idea that she has about mothers-in-law. Nobody can continue to resist somebody who loves them unconditionally. There are things that you can do during her engagement and leading up to the wedding that can begin to break down the barriers and smooth the paths for a wonderful relationship.

My mother-in-law has been my support and [my] spiritual mother. I can always call on her and ask her any question regarding [God's] word. I can count on her to be a wonderful Christian role model and support for me.
—Anonymous

Getting Along With Your Daughter-in-law's Mother

One of the first things that you can do as you prepare to be a mother-in-law is consider that there are other people included in the formula that equals happiness between you and your new daughter-in-law. Assuming that you are the model mother-in-law, perfectly well balanced and secure in every way, there can still be one gigantic (forgive me for calling her that) deterrent to having a great relationship with your daughter-in-law and that is her mother. Whether she is a Christian or not, is close to her daughter or not, is secure or not, no mother wants another woman barging in to take her place. As a mother-in-law you want to be close to your daughter-in-law, so what do you do about her mother and her mother's feelings?

The Do's

The first thing that you do is *pray* and not in the way that you might be thinking. Don't pray that God will strike her mute or that she and her husband will be transferred to another country. There will be none of that. There is a way that God does want you to pray, however.

He wants you to cry out to Him so that He can do something in you that you can't do on your own. Pray for a change of heart so you can love your daughter-in-law's mother. Pray that good will come her way and that God will bless her. Be honest with God and tell Him that you don't feel love for her right now (you may feel the exact opposite) but you are willing to love her if He will help you. Ask Him to help you forgive her for any offensive thing she has said or done. By doing that you are simply releasing your right for retribution or pay back and leaving everything in God's hands. Being willing to love and willing to forgive is a lot easier said than done but the freedom that it brings is worth it.

Your experience with your daughter-in-law's mother may be in a range anywhere from hitting it off right away and being great friends to mild irritation to bitterness or hostility. Regardless of where you are on that continuum of feelings, pray for her. Ask God to give you sympathy, love and compassion for this woman who has genuine concern that she may lose the affections of her daughter to you. Write her name in your journal to remind you to pray. Pray for her by name on a regular basis. Ask God to give her peace and assurance about your relationship with her daughter. Pray that she will be blessed in every way, that good will always come to her and she will know God and His best in her life. If she is a fellow believer in Christ then tell her that you pray for her. Ask if there is any specific way that you can be praying. In doing that, you are assuring her that you only have the best intentions toward her. If she would not be receptive to the idea of you praying for her, just do it on your own without sharing. Both of you will reap the benefits.

Praying for her inevitably leads to loving her. Dr. Jack Graham, pastor of Prestonwood Baptist Church in Plano, TX said, "When we pray we are not trying to change God's mind, (although that has been my motive many times), but we are trying to *find* God's mind." God's mind is that "you must love one another." (John 13:34) We learned from Gary Smalley that love is a decision. That is the next thing you can do to improve your relationship with your daughter-in-law and her mother. Since emotion follows action, purpose in your heart that you are going to *love* your daughter-in-law's mother. Realize that you are on the same team to encourage and help this new couple be the best they can be for each other, for their future family and for God. If you continue to pray and persist in deciding to love, the emotion is much more likely to come along.

The next step to take is to follow up your decision to love her with acts of kindness and thoughtfulness. Give her mother a call from time to time. If you are not a phone person, send a card for birthdays or other special occasions. Write on her Facebook page. Communicate to her what a privilege it is that you can partner together, whether you live close or thousands of miles apart, to be encouragers and cheerleaders in your children's lives. Celebrate and delight with her in every success that she has. Give her genuine compliments (nothing flowery, fake or shallow. She'll see through that in a nanosecond.) Give her builder statements: statements that speak life, encouragement and refreshment into her soul.

Taking these steps to build a positive relationship with her mother is cumulative. One action builds on the next and that one builds on the next; praying for her leads to loving her and loving her leads to being kind to her. All of those things reassure her that you are not out to steal her daughter or her daughter's affections, but you are actually a friend in waiting. Who wouldn't want to be friends with someone like that?

The best thing my mother-in-law ever did for me was give me a wonderful husband and she taught me how to make potato salad.
—Anonymous

The Don'ts

Never speak in an unflattering way about your daughter-in-law's parents, especially to your daughter-in-law. If she is sharing something negative about her folks to you, resist the temptation to join in or agree. She is sure to make up with them later and won't forget your words. If you have something that you think you just have to express or your cheeks will explode, say it to your husband in the privacy of your home where it is impossible for anyone to hear *ever!* It is totally counter-productive to share negative feelings about her family with anyone. Even if you have been hurt or you think something is unfair, stop and think first; "what do I want to have happen in this situation? My goal is to have a good relationship with my son and daughter-in-law. Will what I am about to say bring that about?" I am not implying that you shouldn't say something when you are hurt or that you should never express your feelings. I *am* saying that when you pop off and say something that attacks a person or their character, it works against what you really want to accomplish. Words once said can never be taken back.

Be the grown up. Be hard to offend. Don't criticize. Don't whine. If her parents consistently do those things just listed, then perhaps the contrast between the actions of both sets of parents will be the thing that influences your kids to more readily see your point of view, make good decisions and develop godly character.

Always keep your goal in mind. Your goal is to have a great relationship with your daughter-in-law. A fringe benefit would be to also become friends with her family. After all, you will be thrust together for most of the major events of your grandchildren's lives when they come along. Those times are so much more pleasant when you are all friends.

> *The best thing my mother-in-law ever did for me was helped babysit so my hubby and I could go out on free date nights.*
> —Anonymous

The One in the Middle

The dynamic between the two mothers can be challenging for your daughter-in-law as well. This is particularly true if she is an only daughter and even more if she is an only child.

My eyes were opened when I recently attended a Women of Faith Conference and got to hear the keynote speaker, Patsy Clairmont in a Q and A session. Inevitably when you have several thousand women in one place, you have in-law problems. Patsy was asked how a mother-in-law can have a better relationship with her daughter-in-law. Her response was interesting and gave me a perspective that I had not had before. She said, "You know, sometimes it is very difficult for new brides to try to be close to their mother-in-law because in so doing they experience a feeling of disloyalty to their own mothers."

I had never viewed things from the perspective of a new bride who is close to and afraid to hurt her Momma. (Do you recall earlier I said that there were two things that one needed to be a great mother-in-law and one of those is a good memory? Mine had obviously faded.) The relationship with this new girl in your life is very tenuous because of all of the dynamics that are involved. It can be touchy between you and her mother because her mother may feel like she is being left behind. It can be complicated between your daughter-in-law and you because she doesn't *want* her mother to feel left behind. It can be difficult from your perspective because *you* don't want to be left behind just because you are the mother of the groom. Just being aware of all of these different perspectives can truly help.

> *The best thing my mother-in-law ever did for me was text me to check on me whenever I had a newborn baby. It was so great that she did not call every time since it was such an adjustment. A phone call would have given me just one more thing to do. I would have either had to answer it right then, which would have normally been an inconvenience or would have had to remember to return the call later. Instead, she would just text saying she was thinking about me or wondering how I/we were doing and then I could reply at my convenience or give her a call if time allowed.*
> *—Anonymous*

What Does She Call You?

There is one other important fact that could have an impact on the bride's mother and that is what name your new daughter-in-law calls you. Don't *insist* that your daughter-in-law call you "Mom" or "Mother." It can feel awkward to the bride and very threatening to the bride's mother. It can also reinforce the very feelings of insecurity that we have been discussing. I know that may sound silly, but I have to admit feeling the ping in my heart when I heard one of my sons call his mother-in-law, "Mom." My thought when I first heard it, as immature as it might be was, "Hey! I'm your mother! Why are you calling her Mom?"

Have a discussion about how she will refer to you. Give her some options and even tell her your preference, but let her know that you want it to be something that both of you can be comfortable saying and hearing and you don't want it to be offensive or hurtful to her mother.

> *The best thing my mother-in-law ever did for me was she prayed for me while I was growing up [because] she was praying for her son's wife.*
> —*Anonymous*

Blessing Brunch

Something that you could do in cooperation with your new daughter-in-law's mother is have a "Blessing Brunch" for the bride before the wedding. You can be as creative as you would like as you plan this brunch to offer words of blessing to your son's new wife. I am including a couple of ideas to get you started so you can let your imagination begin to spring into action.

A simple but meaningful "Blessing Brunch" was prepared for Joy by her mother. The next evening she was to be married so she had her bridesmaids stay all night at her home the night before the wedding to have their last girlfriend slumber party. The morning of the wedding, Joy's mother made a lovely brunch for all of them. They ate together and then took turns going around the table praying for the soon-to-be bride as she began this new chapter in her life. There was hardly a dry eye as the girls cried and prayed and shared in this time together. A variation of this type of brunch could be given by the mother-in-law-to-be. The possibilities are endless.

A dear friend of mine decided to have a "Blessing Brunch" for her son's fiancée two weeks before the wedding. She sent out invitations to close friends who had invested in her son and who had prayed for him over the years. The invitation included a plain white notecard. On that card, the guests were asked to write a prayer, special scripture or word of blessing and bring it with them to the brunch to be read to her new daughter-in-law. A lovely meal was prepared, and after they visited and ate, they went around the group and shared their blessings with the new bride. Many just spoke what they had written on the card and others read them. The cards were then given to the bride to keep so that she could reread them when she needed a word of encouragement or just to remember how much she is loved. My friend then read her Mother-in-Law Covenant to her son's fiancée. You will find a copy in the following paragraphs. The morning ended when everyone gathered around and prayed for her future daughter-in-law.

A "Blessing Brunch" is the perfect way to launch the festivities leading up to the wedding. It is an ideal way to officially begin your role as the new mother-in-law. When your daughter-in-law sees you praying for her, blessing her, wishing the best for her and setting her free to be the wife God intended, it dispels any misconceptions and old wives tales that she has heard up until now. When you bless *her,* let go of *him* and then step out of *their* way, you are giving your relationship with your new daughter-in-law and son every opportunity to flourish. *You* will be the one that ends up being blessed.

The best thing my mother-in-law ever did for me was loan us money when we were trying to get out of debt.
—Anonymous

Mother-In-Law Covenant

One of the best ideas that I have seen to start the mother-in-law/daughter-in-law relationship on the right foot was the brain child of someone for whom I have the upmost respect. She is a dynamic Bible teacher and speaker but also a great mother-in-law to her two daughters-in-law. Like me, Marcia Furrow has only boys and knew when her sons got married their wives would take her place as the most important women in their lives. She also longed for a daughter and knew if she mishandled things with her new daughters-in-law, there was the potential that she would have neither sons nor daughters.

Before the wedding of her oldest son, Dan, she wrote a Mother-in-law Covenant to her new daughter-in-law. A Blessing Brunch was planned and at that brunch, Marcia read aloud with all the family as witnesses what she covenanted to do as a new mother-in-law. She signed it while they all looked on and then gave it to her daughter-in-law as a lasting, binding agreement. WOW! That took courage! With her permission, I have included a copy of the covenant below.

> *Blessing Brunch -- April 21, 2007*
>
> *For Nicole Gerald, Soon-to-be Nicole Furrow*
>
> *Nicole, it is my great pleasure to know that you are becoming my daughter. And it is fitting that I am the last one to speak, and that I am speaking right after Gayla, who reminded us of the relationship between Ruth and her mother-in-law, Naomi.*

I want to be the kind of mother-in-law that Naomi was. When Ruth was given the opportunity to leave, and start a new life, she chose to stay with Naomi. Why, because she loved Naomi, not only as her friend, but as her sister in the Lord. Ruth saw, and wanted, the God that Naomi loved.

So, to that end, I am making this covenant with you...

I promise never to put Dan in a position where he has to choose between you and me, whether in discussions, scheduling, family events, holidays, personality conflicts or any other situation that comes up. I promise I will never put him in a place where he must choose one of us over the other.

I will never go behind your back to try and persuade his loyalty to be with me. I will openly communicate with both of you.

I will uphold your relationship with Dan; I will pray that God would continue to strengthen it in Himself. You are the primary woman in his life from now on.

I promise never to undermine your authority in your home. Whether it is in your choice of decorating, menus for entertaining, scheduling, working or staying home, how you clean, when you come and go, or even where you store your dishes, I will not challenge you. Your home is yours and Dan's.

I will uphold your choices and decisions. And, I will encourage you to be bold in exerting your preferences over others.

I promise never to undermine your parenting (should the Lord bless you with children).

I will uphold your authority to raise your children, parent them, school them, and discipline them as the Lord leads you. And, as their grandmother, I will defer to your guidelines, and encourage your children to honor and obey you.

Nicole, I will pray for you, love you, and welcome you into my home, my life, and my heart. I will encourage you, support you, and defer to you in your relationship with Dan, and with your future family with him.

I promise, as your mother-in-law, to try to set the best example of what a Godly woman looks like, so that you will see in me, a mentor, friend, and mother.

I am so blessed to have a daughter!

Marcia L. Furrow

Can you imagine how you would have felt as a young bride to receive a document like this in front of your family and all of those who love you? This would make one feel loved, secure and supported. Remember, no one can continue to resist anyone who loves them unconditionally. In writing and giving her daughter-in-law this covenant, Marcia was doing everything possible to let her daughter-in-law know that she was on her side. Marcia has no intentions of being in a contentious relationship with her dear daughter-in-law and said as much from the beginning.

You can reword and tweak your covenant to fit your particular situation. If it is appropriate or applicable, you may decide to include a sentence or two that addresses your relationship with her mother. Just a brief mention that you promise to never try to tear down, pit your daughter-in-law against or barge in to take the place of her mother would bring great comfort to the bride and to her Mom.

It would take incredible courage and strength to make an unconditional covenant with your daughter-in-law, but what assurance and peace of mind it would give to everyone involved and invested in this relationship. With God's help, you can fulfill it.

The best thing my mother-in-law has done for us is she cares for my family like a wonderful support system, spiritually, emotionally, physically and financially when we need it most.
—Anonymous

Now for the wedding:

Shut up and Wear Beige

"It's not about you." That is the first sentence of Rick Warren's book, *The Purpose Driven Life*. Life is not about me? What a blow! Here's an even harder reality, our son's wedding is not about us either. It's not even about our precious son. The wedding is about them, with an emphasis on the bride part of the "them" (you know that cute, slim, tight skinned girl who is about to become your daughter-in-law). It's her one day to be the absolute center of attention, the princess. Believe me, you don't want to mess with that or it will never be forgotten. In fact, my own mother-in-law told me that a mother-in-law's job on the day of the wedding is to "shut up and wear beige." She didn't literally wear beige at our wedding, but she meant that mothers of the groom were to blend in and go along. They had their day when they got married. Now it is their son and his new bride's turn.

My mother-in-law learned this the hard way. She married an only child and like a lot of only children, he was the apple of his mother's eye. His mother, my husband's paternal grandmother had a little trouble (understatement) sharing, both her son and the limelight. She just couldn't let my mother-in-law have all of the attention. So, on my mother-in-law's wedding day, the one day in her life where she should legitimately have all eyes focused on her, her new mother-in-law made an announcement to the guests at the wedding that she herself was pregnant! That would have made her an expectant mother at a very ripe old age. What do you know? Another Sarah! Talk about sucking the attention away from the bride! Needless to say, she didn't have another child to unseat my father-in-law from lonely only status, but her mission was accomplished. She got the attention she craved and her new daughter-in-law, my mother-in-law shared the hurt with me thirty years later. I believe that is why she believed so strongly in the motto, "shut up and wear beige." She was determined not to repeat the same rudeness and cruelty at our wedding that she received at hers.

The best thing my mother-in-law ever did for me was love me. I have never, ever felt scared or intimidated by her. She has always been there for me. Recently, I lost my Mom to cancer and

[my Mother-in-law] has been wonderful. When referring to her son and I, we're called "the kids". Since my Mom's death, she has been so good to my little brother.
—*Anonymous*

Have it Her Way

At Burger King you can have it your way, but when it comes to your son's wedding, *they* get to choose. They get to decide whether it is inside or outside, what colors they will use, whether the flowers are real or artificial, her dress, the number of guests (there *could* be some compromise on this if you are paying), the number of attendants, formal or relaxed, in a cathedral or at the beach. This is their wedding. You had your wedding and presumably got to pick all of those things. Now it is their turn. I am going on the assumption that your son and she will plan this together, or that he will at least have input, but resist all temptation to offer helpful suggestions or give your creative ideas *unless asked*. Even then be diplomatic and affirm to your new daughter-in-law that this is her day and that she can take or leave your ideas.

It is not uncommon in this era for many groom's families to help financially with the wedding. The more money that is contributed, the more the groom's family (we all know that I mean his mother) feels as though they have *purchased* the right to have things a certain way....namely their way. Hold onto your hat. Don't go there future mother-in-law. You may get your way, but you may also lose your new daughter-in-law before the ink is dry on the Marriage Certificate. The more you communicate to your daughter-in-law-to-be that this is her day and you want to do everything you can to cooperate and make sure it turns out that way, the more you will endear yourself to her right from the start.

I previously referred to Dr. Phil's saying; "Do you want to be right or do you want to be happy?" I have tweaked that saying just a bit when it comes to building rapport with your daughter-in-law to; "Do you want your way or do you want to have a good relationship?" Do you really want to trade getting your way and having the attention that one day for a great relationship with your new daughter-in-law for the rest of your life? Don't be tempted to think that after you get your way and things are to your liking at the wedding that you can make up for it later. Remember, my mother-in-law told me the story about her hurtful experience with her mother-in-law thirty years after the fact.

The best thing my mother-in-law ever did for me was be a wonderful mother to my husband! [She] taught him to do laundry, cook, clean, and work hard!!!
—Anonymous

Do I Get to Do Anything?

So, where can you express yourself during this whole wedding process? It is tradition in our culture that the groom's family hosts the Rehearsal Dinner. You get to pick the venue, the menu, the invites, the music, the flowers, the program and anything else that you would like to have happen in those two hours. It is there that you and/or the father of the groom will have an opportunity to make a speech or offer a toast. Despite the fact that this is your time to contribute to the whole wedding process, you may still want to consult with the bride or at least give her an overview of what you have planned. You don't want to design something that she will absolutely hate. A mother-in-law always has to keep this thought uppermost in her mind; *what do I want to accomplish?* Yes, you have the right to plan the Rehearsal Dinner any way that you would like, but you may want to consider what she wants. I have to repeat myself here; do you want your way or do you want a good relationship with that girl who is going to be in your life until you die? Now there is a thought.

My mother-in-law's generosity is overwhelming, not in a way that is frivolous or with strings attached. The Lord has provided for us through her and we neither take advantage of it nor take it for granted. She gave us our house! She, my husband and my father-in-law built the house we are in and she was able to give it to us now rather than after she died. This has enabled us to live debt free in all areas of our life because we have no mortgage and live within our means on one income. This has allowed me to be a stay-at-home mom and to home school. I guess to generalize for a more far-reaching application, she had a lifetime of wise financial decisions and behaviors that not only taught [my husband] how to handle money frugally but also has given her the freedom to bless people now.
—Anonymous

Your Dress Dilemma

The library is filled with books on who does what at a wedding. You can go to your local library and borrow a book on Wedding Etiquette, but chances are your son's Bride has already checked it out. Traditionally the bride's mother chooses her dress first and gets first dibs on the color of her choice. Life is not fair.

The dress that I was to wear to each of the boy's weddings was very important to me. I understood that the wedding was not about me, but I wanted a dress that made me feel that it was. I longed for a dress in which I looked attractive and above all else, "skinny." My first daughter-in-law told me the color that she wanted me to wear. I loved it, found a beautiful dress and all was good. My second daughter-in-law gave me a range of colors (pastels) from which to choose. My third daughter-in-law went with me and helped me pick out a beautiful dress. Although these were *my* dresses, in all three situations I tried to cooperate with their thoughts and desires and they did the same thing with me. We were able to find something that pleased us all and I must say, I did look very slender at all three weddings. Well, maybe that was due to the fact that I starved myself for weeks before.

What do you do if your new daughter-in-law has drastically different ideas about what you should wear than you do? I have to admit that I would feel very awkward in a western themed wedding where the bride insisted everyone was going to be wearing cowboy hats and chaps. Perhaps that is an exaggeration, but maybe the bride does want you to wear a color that you look horrible in....like orange. You are a summer and everyone knows that summers can't wear orange. This is where all of your diplomatic skills from your children's childhood need to be dredged up. There is a wide continuum of colors that could be called orange. Don't go into panic mode. Just go into a paint store and look at their paint colors strips and you'll see what I mean. Is there a shade of orange that would work for you and for your skin tone? Perhaps peach? You could also talk to your new daughter-in-law about a complimentary color that would look lovely on you and that would blend well with orange. Most brides are not going to be that specific in their requests. She will most likely give you a range of options from which to choose. Be reasonable, pick carefully (nothing too gaudy or flashy to take attention away from the bride), let the bride's mother pick first, involve your daughter-in-law in the process as much as time and distance allow and yes, even pray about dress choice. God has very good taste in clothes.

The best thing my mother-in-law ever did for me was organize a bridal shower for me.
—Anonymous

The Night Before the Wedding

You have your dress, you have planned the Rehearsal Dinner, you have confirmed that he is not going to change his mind, and now it is the evening before the wedding. How can you possibly be a part of making this a memorable (in a good way) and sacred time for your son and his new bride? What can you do to remove any last barriers of insecurity or fear that she may be feeling so that the path is smoothed for the two of you to have an awesome relationship?

Many years ago I was listening to Dr. James Dobson's radio program, *Focus on the Family*. He was interviewing a guest (oh how I wish I could remember who it was) who talked about the importance of a bride's new mother-in-law symbolically setting the bride free to be her own person. The guest suggested writing one's daughter-in-law a letter. I thought that it was such a good suggestion that I filed the idea away in my head. As I was planning and preparing for our oldest son's Rehearsal Dinner I was reminded of that idea. After speaking with my husband, we decided to write each of the kids a letter. I would write one to my new daughter-in-law and my husband would write one to our son. We read the letters to each of the kids at the Rehearsal Dinner so that there would be no doubt on their part of our love and support. The experience was wonderful and meaningful. Following is a copy of the letter that I wrote to my daughter-in-law, Nicole.

>Dear Nicole,
>
>I have a vivid memory of sitting on my bed several years ago thinking, and praying for Matt's wife and trying to imagine what she might be experiencing that day. I remember praying that God would help her in school with any tests or homework that she might be having, even any conflicts with friends that may have come up. I prayed that God would protect her physically, psychologically, socially and spiritually. I asked Him to help her to grow and be strong in her relationship with Him and keep her just for my son. Tomorrow I get to see the answer to that prayer and today I know

that it was you that I was praying for that day and those years before I even met you.

Now that I do know you, I couldn't be happier with Matt's decision to marry you. You are beautiful, fun, hard-working, steady, supportive and kind. You love the Lord and want to be involved in ministry and if that were not enough, you seem to like me too. So Nicole, not only does Matt love you, but Mark and I love you also. You are such a blessing!

As your new mother-in-law I would like to give you something. That thing is freedom. I want to set you free from the baggage a mother-in-law can impose on her poor daughter-in-law. You are free to do your own thing, free to have your own traditions, free to cook and decorate however you'd like, free to have your own tastes and you are free to have Matt. You do not have to do things the way that I do them. I want you to call me the first time Matt says, "My Mom doesn't do it that way" and I will personally yell at him. You are free, Nicole. Free from everything but my prayers. I will continue to pray God's word for you, I will continue to love you and support you (except financially :) and Pops and I will be on the sidelines of your lives cheering with all of our might.

It is with the deepest gratitude to God that we witness not just the beginning of your marriage but the beginning of your ministry together. The day that I began writing this letter I prayed this *scripture for you. "I pray that surely goodness and mercy will follow Nicole all the days of her life and I pray that she will dwell in the house of the Lord forever." May goodness and mercy follow both of you all of the days of your lives as you seek to love and serve Him. Doing that is the only place of real love and joy. I love you and am so grateful for you.*

You new mother-in-law,
Cheryl

Sniff, sniff. Rereading that makes me cry.

You will have to customize your letter to your situation and your experiences with your daughter-in-law as I did when I wrote to the other girls. However, I have learned the wisdom of what I heard that day on Focus on the Family so long ago. Hopefully, that helped the girls not to feel the pressure of having to do things a certain way because I did or clean a particular way (heaven forbid) or cook using the same recipes that I did.

Set her free. It will make your relationship so much better than if you hold onto and try to control things or "help" more than is wanted. What feeling wells up in you when you experience someone grasping onto you or controlling you? It is strangling, intimidating, and stifling. When someone has a grip on you the natural response is to pull away. That is *not* what we want to accomplish as mothers-in-law. We want those girls to be drawn to us not run away from us. Set your daughter-in-law free so that she will willingly, voluntarily come back to you.

The best thing my mother-in-law ever did for me was "help me when my kids were sick. She is a good care giver."
—*Anonymous*

Part 2

Being a Prepared Mother-in-Law

Chapter 5

Those Newlyweds- The Early Years

> "Therefore, as God's chosen people, holy and dearly loved, clothe yourselves with compassion, kindness, humility, gentleness and patience. Bear with each other and forgive whatever grievances you may have against one another. Forgive as the Lord forgave you. And over all these virtues put on love, which binds them all together in perfect unity."
> (Colossians 3:12-14)

"Turn out the lights, the party's over." Can't you just hear Willie Nelson singing that in your head? The party *is* over. Everything has been cleaned up. The guests have gone home and your son and his new wife are on the vacation that you need. Whether you are thrilled with your new daughter-in-law or are feeling something south of that, the deal is done and YOU are a mother-in-law! This is where the real work begins and it begins by showing a little respect.

Hannah's Welcome into Her Husband's Family

Listen to Hannah's story. "After only having been married for two months, we got to spend our first Christmas at my in-laws house in Colorado. There were probably 20 family members at their home that day for a gift exchange. My mother-in-law gave my husband's grandmother a memory book. There were no pictures of me in it, but there was one of my husband and his ex-fiancée. When I started crying and had to excuse myself, my mother-in-law couldn't, and still doesn't, see what she did wrong. My husband asked her to apologize to me, but she has refused."

Hannah's mother-in-law made so many blunders in those few brief moments that it is hard to know where to begin. Her thoughtlessness cracked a fledgling, tender relationship. She obviously did not remember how insecure and vulnerable she felt when she had her first experience with her husband's family all of those years ago. She didn't remember that she wanted to be accepted and validated and made to feel valuable. There is no way that she thought back to her first major holiday away from her parents and how emotional that was. Hannah's mother-in-law not only did not try to empathize, remember and think back, she just didn't think.....period. There is always the possibility that she knew exactly what she was doing. Perhaps her point was to hurt and if that was the case, she succeeded.

On top of being thoughtless and somewhat callous, she refused to understand how Hannah was obviously feeling. The final blow came when she was told about Hannah's hurt and rejected any attempt to repair the damage that had been done. What was she thinking? Did she actually think that things were going to get better from this point on into the years to come? Did she even care?

The whole relationship could have been set aright and the tension defused had Hannah's mother-in-law gone to her immediately and said, "I am so sorry. That was thoughtless of me. Will you forgive me? What can I do to make things better between us?" That would have been exactly what Hannah's spirit needed to hear. Most people are anxious to forgive and live in harmony. A few well-placed sentences could have changed the course of their entire relationship. "A word fitly spoken is like apples of gold in a setting of silver." (Proverbs 25:11 ESV) Unfortunately, that didn't happen.

As the mother-in-law we should, because of our life experience, have more wisdom than our young daughters-in-law. We should be able to take the high road even when we don't think that we are wrong. It does not hurt us to apologize for the sake of the relationship even if we don't understand our mistake. Seek to understand. The implication is not that we become a doormat, but that we show maturity and a humble spirit just as the verses from Colossians at the beginning of this chapter instruct us.

I have been made aware anecdotally about mothers-in-law who set out to destroy the marriage of their son. In some twisted way that type of mother wants to be the only woman in her son's life and will do whatever she needs to do to achieve that. If you feel that way even a little, pray and ask God to forgive you and ask Him to give you His perspective. Ask Him to transform your son's marriage into what He wants it to be and then ask Him to transform you!

The best thing my mother-in-law ever did for me was she helped with my children and housework while I was ill, and, of course, raised a wonderful son, my husband.
—Anonymous

Tricks of the Trade After the Wedding

Respect **Them** and Release **Him**

You must let go of your dear son. His wife is now the most important woman in his life. Let go of your efforts to control. Let go of your longing to mother and baby him. Let go of the dreams that you had for him. Let go of the other girl that he dated that you like better than his wife. Pry your fingers loose and LET GO! Release him to her and into the competent hands of God.

As mothers, we have a long history with our sons; years of nursing him when he was sick, going to so many sporting events and band concerts that we couldn't even begin to calculate the hours; we have kissed his skinned knees when he fell down and worried when he was learning to drive or was out late. When confronted with the idea of turning him over completely to his new wife, I know what you are thinking. "He is *my* son after all. Who knows him better than I do? Has she sacrificed for him the way that I have? How can I release him to her?" That little personal pronoun, *my*, carries with it a connotation of possessiveness. He's mine. But now that he is married he is, and he isn't. He is still your son, but she trumps.

Seinfeld was one of the most cleverly written comedies on television in the 1980s. The writers of that sitcom devoted an entire episode on the subject of "close talking." You've visited with people like that, haven't you? They are the ones that come up into your personal space and get so close to your face when they talk to you that you have to struggle to keep your eyes from crossing as you try to focus. Instead of listening to what they are saying all you can think about is the garlic bread that you ate for lunch. Your immediate impulse is to back up both to focus and to breathe. Backing away is an instinctive reaction.

That same instinct comes to play in relationships that intrude into your personal space. Your impulse, whether conscious or not, is to create some space between yourself and the intruder. That may especially hold true if the intruder is your mother-in-law.

If you come in too close to this new couple physically or emotionally, there is going to be some big-time movement in the relationship and it won't be in the direction that you would prefer. Hanging on to your son and not allowing him to put his new wife first is the same as "close talking" in their relationship. Give their new relationship room to breathe. If you refuse to release him, you are working directly against your goal of having a great relationship with your son and his wife. Smothering him destroys the very thing that you are trying to accomplish, so back off, sister!

The best thing my mother-in-law ever did was raise her son into the man he became. She was a single mom from the time he was about two until he was seven. She was a teacher and although [my husband] and his younger sister were in daycare all day, every day, when she was done with school, she'd pick them up and the three of them would make dinner. She taught them early on how to cook and they both love cooking and entertaining.
—Anonymous

Respect Their Privacy

Sue and Joe live in the same town as Joe's parents. One day they were in the bedroom where Sue was getting dressed and Joe was lying on the bed resting because he had been ill. They thought they heard a noise in the house but dismissed it. Within seconds, Joe's mother stuck her head in the door of their bedroom to find them!!! She came into their house and *walked into their bedroom* uninvited! She was treading on dangerous territory. Under different circumstances, she could have had the shock of her life!

Your son's home is not your home! He and his wife are now their own entity. They are an individual couple separate from you. They deserve respect regarding their privacy because of their marital status. Resist the temptation to check in their medicine cabinet, look at their bills, read their email or open their checkbook just to sneak a peek at the balance. I know this may seem harsh, but this is none of your business. Refrain from looking at price tags or checking in their refrigerator or cabinets. Allow them the privacy that you want and expect for yourself. This snoopy behavior sounds intrusive to most of you, but it happens. And whatever you do, don't go traipsing into their bedroom uninvited. Treat them like the adults they now are.

My mother-in-law is very understanding when we are having hard times. She does not interfere in the relationship...and she even lives next door. She always calls before she comes over.
—Anonymous

Respect Their Way of Doing Things

Brittany went to work one day and when she returned home she found her mother-in-law standing in her kitchen. That was a surprise, but not nearly the surprise that she got as she began looking around her kitchen. Everything had been rearranged. Things on the countertop had changed places or disappeared and the contents of cabinets had been emptied and moved to other cabinets. Nothing was the same as she had left it that morning.

In shock she looked at her mother-in-law, held out her hands and said, "What?!?" Her mother-in-law responded, "This place was such a mess and was so disorganized that I decided that I was going to get it straightened out."

Ouch! In that one act she was letting her daughter-in-law know that she disapproved of her and the way she ran her home. She disapproved of her organizational skills and her cleaning skills. The implication was she didn't even think that Brittany was taking very good care of her husband, the mother-in-law's precious son, either. Insult was added to injury when she explained why she had been so intrusive in Brittany's home.

Let's give this mother-in-law the benefit of the doubt for one minute. There is the chance that she thought that she was helping although her words and actions indicate otherwise. Even if she was trying to help, it only took a couple of hours in one afternoon to tick off several boxes on the list of things that mothers-in-law should never do! She definitely did not respect her married children's privacy, she didn't respect their home, she didn't respect the fact that they have a different way of living; she was intrusive, meddling and cutting, just to name a few of her errors.

Those of you who "get" the whole concept of respecting your children's privacy can still, and probably will, struggle with respecting their way of doing things when they differ from yours. The most loving, caring, good hearted mother-in-law can nearly go off of the rails when she sees her son and his family make a choice that is radically different from the way that she raised him. The difference can be something as simple as being convinced that your son's family eats too much fast food instead of nutritious home cooked meals. It can be that they are slobs and their home looks like a pig sty and that is NOT how you taught him to do things. Perhaps it is the fact that, like Brittany's mother-in-law perceived her to be, they are completely unorganized and you are an organizational freak. On a more serious note, it could be how they handle their money or that they incur too much debt. In many cases, it is something even more philosophically divisive. She may want to be a working mom or bottle feed when you *know* that staying home with the children is best and so is breast milk. It could be that she wants to home school and you believe heartily in the public school system. After all, those people are trained to teach your grandchildren. And hold on gals....this is the big one....what happens when they want to stay home and have their own family Christmas on Christmas morning rather than come to your house to celebrate?

What's a mother to do when you observe some of these differences? You must always be respectful, warm and polite and treat your son and daughter-in-law like the adults that they are. Before you say or do anything, evaluate in your head and not your heart if the thing that is really bothering you is of consequence. The fact that they are slobs or disorganized or eat too much fast food is probably not going to do permanent damage. Always keep in mind that you got to make choices for your family and they are exercising their right to do the same.

I am not a counselor so I can't advise or speak to what you do if you see behavior in your son's home that is truly destructive such as alcoholism, other addictions or abuse of any kind. I can tell you what I think I would do. I would pray and get the counsel of my husband, pastor, other godly people and/or a trained counselor rather than act impulsively. This harmful behavior needs to be confronted and dealt with. Some behavior needs to be brought to the attention of law enforcement. Get good advice on the best course of action to take. I truly hope that the differences that you have with your son's family, and there will be some, are minor and can be worked through by treating this new couple with respect.

My mother-in-law was always there to watch the kids no matter what: when my husband and I wanted to get away, when [I] went back to school, and even when our little ones were sick!
—Anonymous

Bonding Bridge Builders

"Let all bitterness, wrath, anger, clamor, and evil speaking be put away from you, with all malice. And be kind to one another, tenderhearted, forgiving one another, even as God in Christ forgave you."
(Eph. 4:31-32 NKJV)

There are many positive things that you can do to build a bridge to a great relationship with your daughter-in-law. The following example is not one of them.

Jenna was a newlywed and was insecure about most things. A big hole was shot right through what little confidence she had the day she received a cookbook as a gift from her mother-in-law entitled, *Gourmet Cooking for the Lazy Chef!*

Seriously?! Did that woman really see this as building a bridge to a better relationship with her daughter-in-law? That gift was thoughtless and passive aggressive. Fortunately, I know that you are not that kind of mother-in-law or you wouldn't be reading this book.

Be Generous With Compliments

There are many encouraging things that you *can* do to make your daughter-in-law feel comfortable and loved. The first action that you can take is to look for positive things about her and then compliment her. Who doesn't like to hear when they have done a good job preparing a meal or choosing a gift or decorating a room? Some of you may have to look a little harder or be a bit more creative in your compliments than others, but it can be done. If she has you over for a meal and the meat is tough and the vegetables are limp and cold, tell her how nice the table looks. If it is not even set well or there are crusty things stuck to it, compliment her on the lovely candle. No candle? Tell her how comfortable the chairs are. Say something positive and refrain from saying anything negative. I know your mother told you that if you can't find anything nice to say, don't say anything at all, but that doesn't always work with your daughter-in-law. She will know what your silence means. So, find something nice to say and say it.

    I remember the first time that my mother and father-in-law came to visit our new apartment after we were married. I was very nervous because my mother-in-law was quite the cook and I was truly a novice at cooking and housekeeping. I decided to make Kool-Aid lemonade because it was a hot summer day. I made it and served it to them. They smiled and acted delighted with the cool, refreshing drink. They were very kind and affirming about everything. My nerves started to calm a bit and after visiting awhile I went back into the kitchen and poured myself a glass of lemonade. I nearly spewed it out all over the floor. I had put in the water and the drink mix but forgot the sugar. I couldn't get the pucker off of my face for what seemed like hours because of how sour that drink was. I apologized profusely to them when I confessed what I had done. My mother-in-law was so gracious and kind to me that I haven't forgotten it forty years later. When it was time for them to leave, she leaned in and said to me in a soft, smiling voice, "Now, you have the terrible, terrifying first visit from your mother-in-law over with." She didn't say anything negative to me, and she could have. She was warm and complimentary about everything she possibly could be and she let me know that she could relate to the angst that I had been feeling. She did all that she could to set me at ease. You can do the same thing for your daughter-in-law and she will love you for it.

The best thing my mother-in-law ever did for me was accept me warmly and wholeheartedly.
—Anonymous

A Positive Preemptive Strike

Do you want to win your daughter-in-law over in the space of about twenty seconds? Tell your son in front of her that if you ever hear him saying, "This isn't how my Mom makes it," or, "I like the way that my Mom does it better," or anything akin to that, you will personally come and set him straight. In doing this, you are affirming her in her new role. You are letting her know that you have no intention of trying to run his life and that you recognize who the alpha female is in his world. Those few words are establishing who he is to show his allegiance to from the beginning. She knows that she is not going to have to fight you for his attention or approval. I can almost hear her sigh of relief from here.

It takes a very secure person to do this. Deep down inside, we secretly want our sons to think that our mac and cheese or our brownies are the best in the world. If we are not vigilant, there is an ugliness that can rise up within us that wants to compete with her and beat her. Keep your eye on the prize of having a great relationship with your daughter-in-law which is worth so much more than being the best mac and cheese maker this side of the Mississippi.

The best thing my mother-in-law ever did for me was tell her son, my husband, to go home and start behaving.
—Anonymous

Be Aware of Her Culture

Another positive thing that you can do that will help build your relationship with your daughter-in-law is be aware of her culture. You don't have to own an iPhone, an iPad, or a Mac computer. You don't have to be a frequent Facebook user or tweet your day away on Twitter. You can skip the tattoo and the body piercings, but you need to *know* about these things. Listen to the radio, read books, magazines and newspapers, be aware of the popular TV shows and movies that are out even if you wouldn't be caught dead watching some of them. "Be aware" of her culture; don't act like you are a part of her culture. You need to act your age, however, if you know her world and her traditions, you will be able to relate to one another better. If she can relate, that opens up opportunities for conversation which leads to a deeper relationship. If you act like a dinosaur was your contemporary, she will respond to you in the same way. You don't have to be a Pop culture maven, but be able to carry on a conversation about her world.

The best thing my mother-in-law ever did for me was listen and pamper me during my pregnancy.
—Anonymous

Lighten Up

Everyone wants to be around a positive, happy person as opposed to a grumpy, negative one so loosen up and have fun! Don't take yourself so seriously. Have an easy laugh. You don't have to be the center of attention (it's probably better if you are not), but you can enjoy the company of those with whom you are spending time. Get out of the corrective mode of your past parenting and have a good time.

One of the things I love the most about my daughter-in-law, Holly, is that she is so free to be herself. She doesn't feel the need to impress anyone or live up to anyone's standards but God's. I can learn a lot from that girl. I love to have fun, but I can be uptight about some things, like leaving the house in the morning without makeup.

One morning when I was staying with Holly, she came blowing into the bedroom and said, "Come on. We're getting in the car in our pajamas and we're making a run to Starbucks!" "What, without makeup and in our pajamas? I would love a Starbucks, but I need to at least put my clothes on. I can't go out in my pajamas!" Holly looked at me and yelled while she laughed, *"Come on, Nannie! Loosen Up! Loosen Up!!! Let's Go! It will be fun!"* I decided she was right. We loaded into the car in our PJs and made our coffee run.....and it was *fun*! In fact, it was a great memory of a crazy thing that we did together. So the advice is the same to you, *"Loosen Up! Loosen Up! It will be fun!"*

It is also a great way to break down barriers between you and your daughter-in-law.

> *My mother-in-law was the one person who believed me when I said I wanted a teddy bear, even though I was an adult with children of my own. She bought one for me and started my collection.*
> *—Anonymous*

Be Yourself

One more positive thing that you can do to build a bridge to a great relationship with your daughter-in-law is to be yourself and stay within your personality. Some of the previous ideas offered could imply that you need to change who you are. It is not a matter of pretending that you are something you are not as much as having awareness about your traits and being intentional about responding rightly. I can still be uptight. I still don't leave the house in the morning unless I have done the whole makeup and hair thing. I have learned that being positive, not taking myself so seriously and knowing a bit about what goes on in their world opens up the pathway to a better relationship with all of my daughters-in-law. That is worth the effort.

The No-No's

There are a few things that we should never do if we want to build a great relationship with our daughters-in-law. The things that we should avoid don't work and most often backfire on us so why go there?

No Unsolicited Advice

First, do not be in the habit of giving advice. The more unsolicited advice that you give to your son and daughter-in-law, the less they will listen to what you say. The word picture that comes to mind as I think of someone constantly "helping" with their words is that of a Snoopy and Peanuts cartoon special on television. In those cartoons the voice of Snoopy sounds like, "Wah, wah, wah, wah, wah." It is an annoying noise. That's what you will sound like to your son and daughter-in-law if you are forever giving them advice. My own daughter-in-law, Bekah, told me that she wants to ask advice of people who are *not* always giving it. She figures that they are wise enough to keep still until asked and that is the kind of person from whom she really wants to hear.

If you feel like you must let them know your opinion on a particular subject, ask permission to share it with them. Tell them they can take or leave what you have to say, but you would like an opportunity to tell them why you feel the way that you do. By asking them for a hearing of sorts, you are giving them the power as you begin the conversation. When they hold the power, they feel as though they have some control in the situation and are being respected and treated as adults. If after asking them they tell you they just don't want to hear you out, you need to respect that as well. Ok, that's a lot easier said than done, but who ever said being a good mother-in-law was easy?

If they agree to hear your concern, don't blow it by starting any sentence with the emotionally charged words, "You need to," or "You should." The moment those words are said, the defenses come up and it is unlikely that your son and his wife will hear anything else you have to say after that. Just think about what rises up in you when someone approaches you that way. Why not rather say something like, "Thanks for allowing me to tell you what's on my mind," and then state what you have observed. Or, "Have you considered doing _____?" Or even, "Have you ever noticed that when _____?" These types of conversations may become more of an issue when you become grandparents. Invariably your children will make different choices in child rearing than you did. Before you say anything, decide if it is a matter of their personal choice or if it is a matter of genuine concern.

In almost 25 years of marriage, my mother-in-law has never once criticized me in any way – only encouraged and loved me.
—Anonymous

No Interfering in Their Disagreements

Another action from which to refrain is to never, ever pit your son against his wife or manipulate things so that he is put in a position where he has to choose between you and her. The choice has already been made and it was made the day that he said, "I do." Don't go to him when she is not around and say disapproving things about her or try to get him on your side instead of hers on any issue. If something is bothering you about her or them, tell both of them.

Don't meddle in their problems and don't take sides either way if you happen to witness a fight or disagreement. In fact, that is one of the best times to do what your mother used to tell you and, "Zip it!" If you can, leave. Entering into one of their disputes can only break bad on you. Either your son or your daughter-in-law will end up angry with you for taking the other's side. Your choice will also be remembered later when the fuss has died down.

One time when I was spending a few days with my son and daughter-in-law they began having a heated disagreement. At one point as they were arguing back and forth my son looked at me and said, "Mom, what do you think?" What did I think? Was he kidding? I told him there was no way in this world I was going to answer that question. It was lose-lose for me no matter which way I went and it was something that they needed to work out without a word from *his* mother. I know that the tendency is to automatically side with your son, but don't go there mother-in-law. Zip it!

My mother-in-law has provided an amazing example of what a godly mom should be. She raised four godly children and I want to do the same.
—Anonymous

No Command Appearances

This no-no is the hardest for me. If at all possible, don't insist on any "command appearances." Don't demand that they be at your house for Easter, Mother's Day, Fourth of July, Thanksgiving, Christmas or your birthday. Shoot, some Moms insist on their sons being there even for Labor Day. My guess is they want to remind those men of what they, as moms, went through to bring them into the world. I would love to spend every holiday with my sons and their wives, but each of the girls has a family too. Their wants and needs are to be considered as well as my own. I have had to get over the idea that Christmas is on December 25th. Christmas is whatever day that my family can be together. Now, I let the girls talk and see what works best for them and then they tell me the best time for us to get together to celebrate as a family. Things became much more pleasant when I became a little more flexible. I do have to admit that they really try to keep things even between us and all of the other families, and that is a great source of help and comfort.

What good does it do you when you have to force your son's family to come visit you? Do you want someone at your home that doesn't want to be there? The more that you insist and command that they show up on a certain day, the more they will resent it and not want to come for a visit. You may get their bodies, but they will leave their hearts and joy somewhere else.

Do you want to enjoy the holidays, birthdays, Mother's Day, Father's Day, etc? First, be the kind of person that your children would like to spend time with and then show some flexibility. If there is a specific date or time that you want to be together with your children, ask them, don't tell them. When you do that, you are treating them like adults and you are showing them respect. They will in turn respect you and be more likely to come willingly. I admit that all of this is a bit tricky. It takes practice and a lot of communication and prayer to be a good mother-in-law.

The best thing my mother-in-law ever did for me was move the celebration of Thanksgiving to the weekend so I could spend the whole day with my family!
—Anonymous

No "Helping" Without Asking

Sometimes we mothers-in-law genuinely think that we are helping, but our actions are not received as help. I like to sweep floors. I have grabbed the broom many times at my daughter-in-law's home and begun sweeping the floors without asking. I figured that she was so busy with the all of the things that she had to do and the children were so busy tracking dirt and grass into the house that sweeping was a way that I could help. It occurred to me one day that my sweeping could be telegraphing the message to her that I think she is not a good housekeeper or that she is not keeping up with the children well enough. I decided just to ask her straight out. "Does my sweeping help you or bother you? I really want to be of help. There is no way that I could keep up with everything that you do. Is this something that you would like for me to do or would you prefer that I didn't?" Thankfully, she took my sweeping in the way that I had intended and now when I am at her home, I happily sweep on. I would not have known, however if I had not asked.

Once your daughter-in-law has given you permission to do a particular task you don't need to continue to ask every time. You always need to use your God-given common sense. The key in every situation is to try to see things from your daughter-in-law's perspective. Put yourself in her place. Think back and remember. If in doubt at all, ask your daughter-in-law. Had Brittany's mother-in-law handled her actions and words a little differently, the rearranging of Brittany's kitchen could have been a huge blessing to her and not a source of hurt. We have a lot of power in our hands, mother-in-law. Let's use that power to build up and not tear down.

> *The best thing my mother-in-law ever did for me was listen.*
> *—Anonymous*

No Making Your Son the Middle Man

Sometimes when we mothers-in-law want information, help, conflict resolution or a message delivered to our daughter-in-law we take the path of least resistance. We pounce on our son and expect him to deliver the message to our daughter-in-law or give us the information that we are seeking. After all, we have known him longer so we feel more comfortable talking to him. We know him better so we know how he will take it. And, it is the least he could do for us since we went to the brink of death to bring him into this world.

I did this very thing a few months ago. I was talking away on the phone to our son, Matt when out of the blue (I probably was thinking of this book) I said, "Matt. Is there anything that I do that drives Nicole crazy?" There was a two beat pause then he said, "Mom, I think I'll let you have that conversation with her." Did I raise a brilliant son or what? I immediately saw the sense in what he said and told him I thought that was the wisest thing I had ever heard him say. There was no way that my son wanted to get between his wife and his mother. I have to admit I was a little nervous that he just didn't flatly say, "No, of course not." I went scurrying to Nicole pronto to ask what I should have asked her in the first place. You will see her response later in this chapter. It was not bad news, but what if it had been and my son would have been the one to tell me? I probably would have started chirping away at him, nagging to find out more. Nicole may have gotten angry at him for telling me something without her permission or before she had the opportunity to tell me herself. By asking Matt the question that I should have been asking Nicole, I was putting him in an awkward, no-win situation. I'm so glad that he was wise enough not to let me get away with it.

Don't put your son in the middle. Don't ask him questions about how your daughter-in-law feels about certain things. Don't ask him why she doesn't like you or what she is upset about. Don't make him deliver messages, and don't say things to him that you want to get to her but don't have the courage to say to her yourself. Don't ask him to do your dirty work. As the older and hopefully more mature person, you need to model adult behavior. The more open and honest your communication is with your daughter-in-law, the more she will trust you. She will have confidence that you will never undermine her to her husband and she'll always know where she stands with you. That equals security. Behavior that is up front like that will lead to a growing, flourishing relationship with your daughter-in-law. Your son will love you for it too.

One of the most helpful things that my mother-in-law ever taught me was to always have the table set every evening when my husband gets home. Even if I don't have a clue what I am going to make for supper, he will see that I have at least thought about it and it enables him to wait more patiently.
—Anonymous

Mother-in-law Meter

May I offer one final suggestion for all mothers-in-law during the first, tenuous weeks and months after our sons and wives are married? They are not only new at their marriage but we are new at being mothers-in-law. Most of the time, we don't know what we are doing in our new role any more than they do. We don't know if we are doing things that are being received well or poorly so we need to find out. After a few months, take your daughter-in-law to lunch or to some activity that you both enjoy and ask her how you are doing as a mother-in-law. Ask if there is anything that you could or should do differently. Let her know that your goal is to have a great relationship with her and you want to do the best that you can to be a loving, supportive mother-in-law.

I asked my daughter-in-law, Holly, this question several months after she and Chris were married. She told me that, yes she did have a suggestion for me. There was something that I could do if I wanted to be a better mother-in-law. I gulped and listened and braced myself much like they do when I give them my well placed words of advice. She told me that she would like it if I called more. It seems that my distance and effort to give them lots of space in their new marriage was coming across as being uncaring and unconcerned. I was shocked. I had no idea that she felt that way but was so grateful that she let me know. Now that I know, I can do something about it. That negative impression that was developing about me didn't have time to incubate and become a full blown hurt that was beyond repair. I am very glad that I asked and I'm extremely grateful that she had the courage to tell me.

Each person interprets and processes things differently, so you cannot assume that what bothers one of your daughters-in-law will bother the other. You also can't assume what speaks love to one will communicate love to the other. I will admit that by my third daughter-in-law I was growing a little complacent and figured that with all of my experience surely I was at least in line for Mother-in-law of the Year. As I was writing this chapter it occurred to me that I had not asked Nicole if there was anything that I could do differently. Remember, I asked Matt first. I needed to fix my mistake. We were driving together one day and I said to her, "You know, Nicole, I've been thinking about this and I was wondering if there is something that I do that makes you crazy or hurts your feelings or is insensitive in any way." She sat there for a moment and I knew that she was afraid to say what was on her mind. I said, "I'd like to know because I can't change anything that I don't know about." Finally she told me that I always seem to be in a big hurry to get off of the phone when she calls and it comes across like I am uninterested or too busy to bother talking to her. I told her I thought that she had a valid point. I *am* always in a hurry to get off of the phone but not just with her but with everyone. I hate chatting on the phone. I am just *not* a phone person. When she realized that about me, she knew it wasn't personal. When I heard what I was doing and the message I was giving to her, and probably everyone with whom I spoke on the phone, it was eye opening. I did not want to come across that way. I don't want anyone, especially my daughter-in-law to feel like I am giving them the bum's rush. That little conversation with her has made me much more conscious of how I treat people when I am on the phone. Again, I would never have known had I not asked.

Pray and then muster the courage to ask your daughter-in-law how you are doing or if there is something that you could be doing better. Let her know that whatever she says will be well received. Reassure her that this is not a trap but a genuine effort on your part to do the very best that you can to be a great mother-in-law. Then listen, don't talk. Try with everything in you not to be defensive. Repeat back what she has said to show her that you were listening and then thank her for being honest with you. Really pray about and mull over what she has told you. Change whatever is reasonable so that you can be the mother-in-law that God intended you to be.

The best thing my mother-in-law ever did for me was have conversations with me about deep issues.
—Anonymous

Still Hitting and Missing?

Sometimes you just don't know the right thing to say to your daughter-in-law. It's not because you dislike her, in fact, you love her but the right words aren't there. When you do say something, it is wrong. You find yourself longing to hear certain words from her as well, but they don't come. It's as if you both are on a tennis court and one serves and the ball lands wide then vise-versa all of the time. Back and forth, miss after miss. You have asked her how you can be a better mother-in-law and her response is, "I wish we could communicate better." What does that mean and what does that look like? You don't know and she may not be able to tell you.

The father and son in the movie, *We Bought A Zoo*, had the same problem. The movie starred Matt Damon as the dad, Benjamin Mea and Colin Ford as the son, Dylan Mea. After the death of his wife and Dylan's mother, Benjamin Mea bought a struggling zoo and moved his family away from the home they knew to begin this new adventure and give them all a new start. He made the assumption that it would be good for everyone. It didn't quite work out that way. Distance and resentment grew between this father and son. They found that they were not communicating, not meeting one another's needs and were drifting farther and farther apart. One night in exasperation they had this conversation:

> The son, Dylan Mea: "I never know what to say to you."
>
> The father, Benjamin Mea: "I'm the same way. *Why don't we tell each other what we wished the other guy would say?*"
>
> (They both smile.)
>
> The son, Dylan Mea: "I'm sorry I brought you to the sticks."
>
> The father, Benjamin Mea: "You're a great dad."
>
> (They both laugh)

This could be an effective way to begin the conversation with your daughter-in-law. Just be honest and say that it seems no matter how hard each of you tries, your words seem to be glancing off of each another. You never know what to say and you are guessing that she feels the same way. Simply ask her, "Why don't we tell each other what we wished the other would say?" If both are willing, having that conversation could give you real insight into the heart of the other. You would know what she needs to hear and then you can say it. It is a start in building authentic communication between the two of you.

Another quote from that movie is, "Sometimes all you need is twenty seconds of insane courage." The twenty seconds it takes to ask your daughter-in-law to have that conversation with you might take insane courage, but it might pay off insane dividends if your daughter-in-law and you understand each another better.

Finally, the relationship between you and your daughter-in-law has fallen into a nice rhythm. You understand each another so much better now. It is only natural that your mind turns to other things, like grandchildren! What are they waiting for?

My mother-in-law taught me so many things about my husband since she had lived with him so long and knew him so well. I learned to ask her questions quite frequently like, "Why would he spend money on a game such as golf?" My father had inexpensive hobbies like gardening and fishing. She very quietly responded that when he gets away to play golf, he will come back a better father and husband and he did.
—Anonymous

Before the Grandchildren

"Fathers [and Mothers], do not provoke your children to anger by the way you treat them....."
(Ephesians 6:4 NLT)

I have often wondered why, in God's plan, menopause usually accompanies the departure of our children from our home. It just doesn't seem right. Not only do our adult children leave, but our good senses leave as well. Everything moves out. One moment we can be totally calm and clear thinking and then the next, look out! This rapid retreat of hormones within our bodies causes us to do and say things that we would have been appalled to even think about just a year ago. Because of this chemistry cacophony going on within us, we must especially be on guard when it comes to what we say to our married children. Believe it or not, menopause does not give anyone license to let it all out.

Not only does menopause mess up our minds and bodies, but every hot flash is a reminder of our own mortality. We become sensitive when we ponder the fact that we are not getting any younger and neither are our kids. They need to start thinking about having a family. Can't they see that career is not everything? Can't they see that circumstances will never be perfect? Can't they see our need to be grandparents while we can still move?

The combination of this longing within us and the hormones talking is that we begin to drop uninvited hints to our married kids that it is time to start thinking babies. We open the discussion with a subtle question like, "When do you think you would like to start a family?" Never mind they already have one started with the two of them. Or there is the popular, "Did you see that Tom and Jenn had a baby? You were in the same class in school, weren't you?" As time goes on and there is no prospect of a grandbaby on the horizon, statements become a little more to the point. "What are you waiting for?" "You are not getting any younger, you know." "I would like to at least see my grandchild before I die."

If someone hounded you like that or pressured you to do something, how would you respond? Would you think to yourself, "Oh my word! I never thought of that! I better put that on the calendar right away?" Or, would your reaction be more resistant because of the nagging and attempt at coercion and control? When mothers-in-law keep coming at their grown children and pluck the same string over and over, it is not only wearing, but it is counterproductive. It will more than likely make your children pull away and become secretive with their plans. Your persistent reminders just may make them dig in their heels and maybe even put off having children even longer. No one likes the feeling of having someone try to exert control over them. That is especially true of our adult offspring. This is just too big an issue in which to meddle.

The very best thing that you can do is button it up and let them live their lives and make their decisions as to when they want to make you a grandmother. Trust them to make the best decision for them and trust God to work everything out according to what is best for everyone. The anticipation will make the event even sweeter. In the meantime, take some hormones or take a nap.

The best thing my mother-in-law ever did for me was that she thought highly of my opinions.
—*Anonymous*

Infertility Issues

Megan wanted nothing more than to be a mommy. She and Mike had been married for seven years and had been trying to get pregnant for most of those years. She had gone through four in vitro-fertilizations with no success as well as several series of shots that lasted up to forty days in a row. She was exhausted mentally, physically and emotionally. Megan's mother-in-law was aware of everything that Megan had been through, but her words of wisdom were, "Just relax and have more sex and you'll get pregnant."

Megan sarcastically thought, "Oh great! Sure! Now that's something that never occurred to me!" Her mother-in-law's insensitive words did nothing but pile onto the hurt and feeling of failure that Megan was already experiencing.

Finally, Megan and Mike were given the news that it was going to be impossible for Megan to have a biological baby because her fallopian tubes were completely closed from scarring. That information was devastating to this young couple. After a period of time they came to grips with that truth and began to seriously pursue enlarging their family through adoption. They took Megan's mother-in-law out to dinner one evening to break the exciting news to her that it looked like they were going to be able to get a baby from Korea. Her mother-in-law looked at her and said, "I just can't accept that my son is not going to have his own child." Megan was so crushed by her mother-in-law's words that she ran out of the restaurant crying.

Infertility issues are too huge to even begin to address here so we aren't going to try. Our focus is how a mother-in-law can be supportive and helpful when our kids are dealing with being unable to get pregnant. Letting them know all of the time how badly we want to be a grandmother does not help. Megan's story shows us that our words and actions can have a shattering effect.

Mother-in-law, your words have real power; power to heal or power to destroy your daughter-in-law and any hope of a good relationship with her. Those careless words from Megan's mother-in-law caused hurt that impacted their relationship until her dying day. Think before you respond. Send up an arrow prayer, the kind that you quickly shoot to heaven for guidance before you utter a word. Mentally relate to your daughter-in-law and how you would feel if you had experienced the same grueling events that your daughter-in-law has just been through. Pay attention to her emotion and respond accordingly. Let your words be those of encouragement and building up. Listen to her, cry with her, pray with her and always reassure her of your love for her. Ask her what you can do that will be the most help to her. That is the kind of person with whom your kids will *want* to share. If you respond in that way, you will be among the first to whom they reveal all of the important events in their lives.

Having children is a very personal and delicate matter in any couple's life. It is best if we mothers-in-law just leave the whole baby making business up to our kids. Feel free to express every feeling and emotion you have about the situation to God and trust Him for the rest. Like everything else in our lives, He gets to choose, and He always chooses best.

The best thing my mother-in-law ever did for us was let us move in with her at a really hard time in our lives.
—Anonymous

Chapter 6

Did You Call Me Grandma?

> "Children's children are a crown to the aged, and
> parents are the pride of their children."
> (Proverbs 17:6)

There is no experience quite like being a grandparent! It is fun, humbling and awe-inspiring all rolled together. It brings extreme joy, but grand-parenting also brings a terror that we may not have experienced with our own children. When we were young parents, we were naïve and lacked the life experience to become as frightened as we now can become over those fragile, incredible little people. Ignorance was bliss.

On the other hand, being a grandparent provides the reality that a part of you will continue after you are gone. It is through that new grandchild that you can obtain a bit of immortality. What a thrill to see your eyes or your hairline or your family's skin tone reproduced in that small human being. Yes, being a grandparent evokes intense feelings of love and pride.

There is something else those wee ones can bring out in us if we are not vigilant. The birth of a grandchild can cause one to have a competitive, self-centered, me first attitude, especially with the other set of grandparents. Embodied in that little person are two whole families melded together, and there's the rub. It is easy to think that our family's way is better, our taste is better, and our genes are better. What can be done to combat these natural, fleshly inclinations?

As a mother-in-law, there are many things to consider when you become a grandparent. Two of those issues are how you will relate to and deal with your adult children who are now parents and how you will behave toward and react to the other set of grandparents. Let's explore the relationship with the other set of grandparents first. You have the power, depending on how you respond to this new dynamic, to make this a joyful partnership with the other grandparents or to make it one in which your children are sandwiched in a contentious situation between both sets of grandparents.

The best things my mother-in-law ever did for me was love me and tell me that I was a wonderful mother.
—Anonymous

Your Relationship with the Other Grandparents

The first thing that can be done is to determine that, at least from your side, you are going to have an alliance with the other grandparents. Look out for their interests and concerns with the grandchild that you share as you do your own. Take opportunities to tell them what a privilege it is to partner with them in praying for this blessing that God has given both of you. Share. Share the baby, share pictures, share stories, share cuddling time. Respond to the other grandparents like Christ wants every follower of His to respond, with love, consideration, thoughtfulness and care.

Our son, Chris is the oldest of our three boys. He married Holly who is from a family of three girls. Chris and Holly had our first grandchild which happened to be another boy. My friend Linda, Holly's mother, had raised three girls so she got to be the first to hold our grandson. When our kids had their second child, they had a beautiful girl. Since I had been girl deprived my entire life, Linda looked at me and insisted that I hold our granddaughter first. Those simple acts of considering the wants and needs of the other bonded us as a team. Now we stand together on the sidelines to root for our kids as they parent our grandkids.

Perhaps you don't have a great history with the other set of parents and the bad blood goes as far back as your kid's courtship. Don't despair because there is still hope. A new grandbaby can bring a new beginning. Go to her parents and apologize for any part that you have played in the rift. Tell them that you would like to have a new start as your grandchild begins a new life. Make clear your desire to be on the same team. There will be no one happier for your decision in the short term than your own children and no one will benefit more in the long term than your grandchild.

It is even more probable that the two sets of grandparents just don't know each other well. This is a perfect time to initiate a friendship. Remember, it is very likely that you will be with these people at every important event in your grandchild's life from here until death do you part. Tell them of your desire to be allies as you support and encourage your children in their new role as parents. Do all that you can do to establish a friendship with them.

One of the best ways that you can enhance the bond with the other set of grandparents is to refuse to compete with them.

Despite how horrible it sounds, competition between the two sets of grandparents happens and can be so subtle that you are knee deep before you even realize it. The best intentioned grandparents can get tied up in keeping up. To keep from looking bad, you have to go one better than they did. Her parents buy your new grandchild a new baby bed so it is only natural for you to feel the pressure to come up with a costly gift too. They spend a certain dollar amount at Christmas time and you must do the same. After all, you don't want to look like you don't care, or that you are cheap, or you don't have the money. While you are participating in this game, you are often not even aware that you are competing. You convince yourself that you just want to give your grandchild the same experiences that the other grandparents are giving him or her. After all, what if your grandchildren end up liking them better?

It takes a disciplined person to spend only what they can afford. It takes a wise person to know when enough is enough. It takes a mature person to restrain herself from trying to buy the love of her children and grandchildren. It takes the help of God to possess those qualities and apply them. Examine yourself. Pray and ask God to show you if you are entangled in competitive behavior. If you need a tangible way of keeping track of expenditures on your grandchildren so that you can control your spending, keep a journal of the money that you spend. Seeing your costs in black and white can help you see the reality of actual dollars spent and be a reminder to control the bent to compete. Even though these rivalries are usually unspoken, your grandchildren will sense them, use them to their advantage and may end up imitating them. A "keep up with the Joneses" lifestyle is not what you want to model or teach your grandchildren.

Another way to live out godly behavior in front of your children and grandchildren and enhance the partnership with the other grandparents is to always speak positively about your daughter-in-law's parents. They may be driving you crazy. You might be the only one in the equation who is trying to treat grandparenting as a partnership. You may even be the only one acting like a grown-up, but don't give in and say what you are thinking. Even if your daughter-in-law is popping off about her parents and you would enjoy nothing more than to join in, don't. What goes out of your mouth can never be taken back and it is unlikely that it will ever be forgotten.

Instead, use every opportunity to say an upbeat, affirmative word in regard to her parents. This especially holds true as you refer to them while speaking to your grandchild. When you talk in positive ways about their other grandparents, you are modeling the very behavior that you want your children and grandchildren to exhibit. If you are in a difficult situation with the other set of grandparents, your good reactions will make a positive impression on your grandchildren. After all, your grandkids are some of the most brilliant children ever born. They will see a disparity in the way that you act compared to their other grandparents if they are acting negatively. Hopefully, the winsome way that you respond will have an impact for good on both your grandchildren *and* their other grandparents.

The final idea is redundant, but it can't be said too often. Pray. Pray for her parents. Pray that God will bless them and bring good to them. Pray that they will grow in their relationship with Him. Pray that they will be wonderful examples as grandparents. If you know of specific needs, pray about those. My daughter-in-law, Bekah's mother Renea, called us the week before we left to go see Jon and Bekah in Ethiopia. She wanted to let me know that she had already begun praying for us. They had just arrived back in the United States from Ethiopia and knew what we would be facing in our travels and what the living conditions would be. She told me that she would be praying every day that we would stay healthy and do well. I felt her support and encouragement as we prepared to leave and during our trip. That kind of kinship is priceless.

Praying for your daughter-in-law's parents also helps to bond you together. My youngest daughter-in-law, Nicole's mother, Joy, is a pastor of a church. Every Sunday morning I try to pray for her as she prepares to get up before her congregation. It is a huge responsibility to speak for God and I want to be one who supports Joy through prayer. Relating to her and praying for her every Sunday morning makes me feel closer to her.

I admit it is harder to pray for the other set of grandparents when things are difficult between you. If things are touchy with the other grandparents, God has the power to change a bad relationship. You simply cannot maintain a horrible attitude about someone for whom you consistently pray. Through prayer God begins to show you His heart for that cantankerous person. He usually reveals to you that you are not very different from them.

If you are in a great relationship with the other set of grandparents, God can make it even better as you pray for them. Pray that God protects that relationship and that the enemy is not allowed to cause a fissure between you.

When you live in real partnership with the other set of grandparents, it is a gift from God to you, to your children and to your grandchildren. Resolve within your heart and mind that you will join the other grandparents to root for and be godly examples for your shared grandchildren.

> *The best thing my mother-in-law ever did for me was tell me about Jesus. I wouldn't be a Christian today if it weren't for her. She asked me to go to Bible study many times when I had no interest in going but she didn't give up. She kept praying and kept asking me until I finally went and learned about Jesus and knew that He was what I wanted and needed in my life. Now I lead a Bible study of 150 women and children and no one is happier for me than my mother-in-law.*
> —*Anonymous*

Your Response to Your Children Who Are Now Parents

It is understood that the news that you are going to be a grandparent is not always good news. Sometimes your son gets things out of order and your grandchild comes before there is a wedding. But, every baby is a precious gift from God, created in His image and that baby is *not* responsible for how he or she got here. Your new grandbaby, despite the circumstances of their arrival, needs to be treated with the same love, dignity and care that Christ Himself would give them. They didn't do anything but come into the world and it is now your responsibility to love and value that dear child.

What do you do if your children don't do things God's way and the girl your son is dating gets pregnant perhaps without even a hint of a wedding? I have not had this experience so I feel uncomfortable giving advice without having been in that position. I can tell you this, however. How you respond now will set the tone for your relationship with your son and his girlfriend and has the potential to affect your relationship with your new grandchild.

I inquired of some very learned people as to the best course of action if you find yourself in this situation. Their advice was that there are a couple of things to keep in mind immediately before a word is uttered from your mouth. First, the baby is God's creation and is to be loved and valued as so. Second, don't reserve blame solely for the girl who might end up being your daughter-in-law. It took two to make that baby and your son was a willing accomplice. It would be best if you and your husband could sit down with both of them to talk about the baby, their plans and their future. In all likelihood, your son already knows that you are going to be disappointed when he gives you the news. Your discussion at this point will be determined by your son and his girlfriend's demeanor and attitude. Do not harass, belittle or harangue. That will only serve to drive them away and may keep you from having a relationship with your grandchild. Remind them that God values all life and has a plan for this new little one that He has allowed to be conceived. Ask what their plans are; if they have explored the option of adoption, are keeping their baby, or are marrying. Let them know that your plan is to love your new grandbaby and his or her mother and as well as your son. You will try to be a source of strength and encouragement and you will always be praying for all of them. If you feel it is appropriate and would be helpful, you can let *him* know how saddened you are *once*. A disapproving word to your expected grandchild's mother may never heal so that is not recommended. Finally, let him know that this is the only time that you are going to say your piece about the *circumstance* of your grandchild's birth. Then you have to keep that promise.

Your response is critical! If your son and his girlfriend are not believers, you have the opportunity to show them how followers of Jesus act in crisis. You can be the one to show them love even when you are disappointed. Your situation may be so difficult that it will take an act of God in your life to love the mother of your grandchild. Pray and draw on God's strength to do in you what only He can do. He can cause you to love your grandbaby's mother. This girl now holds the power as to whether you will have a relationship with your grandchild. Although she is not technically your daughter-in-law, you want to do all that you can to maintain a great relationship with her and maybe, by the grace of God, she *will* be your daughter-in-law and you *will* have a lasting, wonderful relationship.

I realize this is a very simplified answer to an extremely complex question. No two situations are alike so pray, read God's word for wisdom, seek godly advice and perhaps even see a qualified Christian counselor to help you deal with your feelings and responses in the proper way. God is in the business of redeeming and restoring. That's what He does best. He can redeem this circumstance and bring great blessing from it. The greatest blessing is likely to be that precious grandbaby!

My mother-in-law taught me to be careful in what my husband and I said in front of our children. She encouraged us to share everything with each other but to be very cautious about what we say in front of the children that might belittle, tear down or be critical of someone outside of our family. Not that we didn't realize there were negative issues in their home but she always focused on the positive.
—Anonymous

How Should a Mother-in-law Respond When Her Grandchild is Not Physically Perfect? (According to the World's Standards)

Kathy and Doug both knew that God wanted them to go overseas and work with people of other cultures long before they met each other. Separately, each had a deep longing to share their skills, their love, and especially Jesus with people who were very different from themselves. Kathy completed medical school and residency and had already done a short term mission in a third world country when she met Doug. He had traveled the world and was proficient in Russian. It was a match made in heaven. Within six months they were married and were aggressively pursuing their life's call. Moving to Russia became their focus and goal. However, every time they had things in order to go, Kathy would get pregnant and they would have to put off their departure a bit longer. Three babies later they finally had the arrangements made when Kathy found that she was pregnant with baby number four. They were optimistic and knew they could do it with four children and God's help. The time was drawing near when they could pack up the children and finally get started living out their dream.

When their fourth child was born, however, she had a cleft palette. Since Kathy was a doctor, she knew how to care for baby Amber and her special needs. After a few months their precious little daughter began having horrible seizures. It became evident that their deep desire to go to another culture was going to have to be delayed again, this time for many years. Their daughter was going to require much more extensive health care than they could get for her in a foreign country.

Quickly they experienced the heartache and angst of a disabled daughter and the death, or at least severe wounding, of a dream.

Kathy's mother-in-law lived half way across the country but still managed to be an incredible source of encouragement and strength for Kathy. She let Kathy call her to talk, vent and share. She listened without judgment. Kathy was able to tell her mother-in-law good news or bad concerning Amber and she was always attentive and compassionate. While others didn't want to hear any of the bad news, Kathy's mother-in-law listened. She also was a pray-er. Any concern that Kathy had, her mother-in-law would take to heart and take to God. Kathy felt her mother-in-law's support and knew she could call her or go to her whenever she needed to, in good times or bad.

As grandparents, we never want to see any of our family members suffer, especially our children or grandchildren. If our grandchild is not born physically or mentally perfect according to the world's definition, the natural response is to be heartsick and saddened. We know that pain, difficulties and sheer exhaustion are our kid's and grandchild's future. We understand life is going to be more challenging and demanding than any of us thought. And we know that when they hurt, we hurt. That's not how it was supposed to be, but that is how it is.

So, how can we be good mothers-in-law in times like these? Enter into our son and daughter-in-law's pain. As a mother, I want to make things better for my children. In trying to accomplish that, there have been times when I have added to their distress and hurt. One of our grandchildren was going through a physical difficulty. As my son was relaying to me the news the doctor had given them at their last appointment, I said, "On the bright side", and then added a trite little sentence. My intent truly was to make him feel better. His response to me was, "Mom. No offence, but I don't want to hear the bright side." What he and my daughter-in-law needed more than anything was for me to empathize with them. They needed to hear from me how sorry I was that this was happening to them and to our grandchild. They needed to have their feelings affirmed that this whole situation really stinks. After I entered into their pain, empathized with them, sat with them, was there for them, then I could earn the right to point them to scripture and prayer and to God who entered into their agony by coming to this earth to die in their place and mine.

Don't slap a Bible verse or a trite religious saying on your suffering son and daughter-in-law. To them, it feels like smashing a Band-Aid onto a broken arm. It adds to their ache.

In all likelihood your son and daughter-in-law are physically, emotionally and spiritually drained. There is also the possibility that your daughter-in-law may blame herself for the fact that her child is not perfect. If she would have gotten more rest, if she would have eaten better, if she would have seen the signs earlier, perhaps something could have been done for her baby. You may be as distraught as your kids are about your grandchild, but this is the time to rise to the occasion. Assure her with your words and actions that your new grandbaby has real value, purpose and is a blessing from God. Pledge to pray for your daughter-in-law that God will give her strength and wisdom to know how to deal with each challenge as it arises. Let her know that you will faithfully be praying for your grandchild. Ask how you can be of specific help. She might be so overwhelmed with this curveball that life has thrown her that she may not be able to think clearly enough to formulate a request. Have a list of things ready that you are prepared to do when you talk to her so that she won't have to think, nor will you. Ask, "Can I bring over a meal? May I watch the other children while you take a nap? Do you need anything from the grocery store? Can I do your laundry? If you are comfortable with the idea, I can change the sheets on the beds. Would you like a Starbucks?" You get the idea. You have a good guess what your daughter-in-law needs, but the ball must be in her court. She gets to choose even how you help her because unwanted help is not help. Don't run away. Often it is easier to remove ourselves from difficult situations rather than get in there and help bear the load. Remember, our reactions to the difficult things in life are going to be what speaks to our kids the most. Love your daughter-in-law through this. Lend a listening ear without judgment when she speaks to you. Assure her that you don't blame her if she confesses to you that she harbors feelings of blame. If she doesn't mention it, don't you mention "blame." You may place an idea in her head that she didn't have and the mere fact that you brought it up may make her think that you have had those thoughts about her.

Speak to and treat this baby like you do your other grandchildren. Value and love this child and watch to see how God uses this baby to bring light and life into all of your lives.

***The best thing my mother-in-law ever did for me was
love my children.
—Anonymous***

Gram-in-law Gaffes
Don't Expect your Kids to Parent Like You Did

Let's get back to the run of the mill issues with which every grandmother-in-law has to deal. Number one on the list would have to be the discipline or lack thereof of our sweet grandchildren. We are usually convinced that our kids are either too lenient with our grandkids or too hard on them. Your adult children's way of discipline may range anywhere on the scale from putting your grandchildren in timeout to giving them a swat on the backside. They may talk to your grandchildren about their feelings concerning a certain task or perhaps they tell them to, "Do it because I said so." They may ignore bad behavior, give in just to end the confrontation or they may ground your grandchild until they are eighteen. This is not to advocate any of those ways of discipline, but it is to say that your adult children get to choose. They get to decide how they want to raise and correct their own children and it is our job to support them unless you observe abuse. This is where things get really hard, but we should not give any advice concerning discipline or child-rearing unless asked. Remember, the less that we volunteer our opinion the more likely our adult children are to ask us for it.

There is a deep seated insecurity inside of nearly every young mom about the way she is dealing with or rearing her children. There is a fear that if she does it wrong, her children will end up in a juvenile detention center by the time they are in sixth grade. The insecurity seems to be especially keen when her mother-in-law is looking on.

I was surprised to find in the surveys that I received back from daughters-in-law that one of the most given responses to the question, "What one thing does your mother-in-law do that drives you over the edge?", were answers like; "[she is] critical of my mothering, judges my parenting, [and] passive aggressive when trying to interject about parenting my children, her grandchildren, and, [she does] not understand or listen to the definition from our doctor of a legitimate hyperactive grandchild." All of this "help" given by mothers-in-law was received as hurt. Mostly what it accomplished was driving a wedge further between the mother-in-law and her daughter-in-law. Unless there is something dangerous happening to your grandchildren, the best thing that mothers-in-law can do is pray and support your son's family wherever possible. The first gram gaffe is, expecting your daughter-in-law to parent like you.

My mother-in-law did not question my parenting (at least to my face) and she is a great grandma. My daughter loves her.
—Anonymous

Compliment Her Parenting Skills

The response to the question of the survey that read, "What one thing could your mother-in-law do to improve your relationship?" was not surprising. The answer many times over was, "compliment my mothering." Buttoning our lips may keep us from hurting our daughters-in-law, but our words of affirmation can help build them up. They need to hear that they are doing a good job whether they are a stay-at-home mother or a working mom. If your daughter-in-law is a stay-at-home mom, mothering is her career and everyone needs positive words and encouragement in their careers, especially when it is in a job as important as bringing up your grandchild. The working mom also needs your encouragement because she faces pressures of a different kind. Maintaining a career may energize her and perhaps make her a better parent, but she still requires support from those around her. She may love her profession but she probably has moments when she feels she is not doing a very good job at work or parenting. Those mothers need to hear a kind, uplifting word from us as well. Then there are mothers who are forced to work outside of their home because of a sluggish economy or financial problems. It would not be their first choice. If that is the case, guilt can be overwhelming. They definitely don't need us piling on.

A few years ago I was in Atlanta helping my daughter-in-law, Bekah, clean their condo in preparation for it to be sold so they could be on their way to Ethiopia. After a long day of doing the myriad of last minute things that are required to move out of the country, my granddaughters were over it and my poor daughter-in-law had had it. Bekah had just disciplined my rambunctious five-year-old granddaughter and she looked like she was about to crack. I looked at her and said, "Bekah. There is one thing that I have noticed about your parenting skills." I could visibly see her stiffen and I knew she was bracing herself for some *constructive criticism*. My real fear was that she was balling up her fist behind her back to let me have it. I heard tension in her voice when she said, "*What?*" I told her, "You are a much better mother than I was and you are doing so much better than I ever did." The girl almost turned to jelly right before my eyes. She went from a posture of defensiveness to immense relief. It was at that moment that I realized that the words I use to my daughters-in-law have the power to bring blessing or bludgeoning. Because of the way the day had gone and all of the stress that Bekah was experiencing, she needed to hear that she was doing a good job as a parent and she *was*. She was so patient with the girls and I could see her persistence, patience and restraint even if she could not.

Look for whatever positive thing that you can find about your daughter-in-law's parenting skills and mention it. Tell her especially in stressful times. She needs that reassurance from you. What motivates you to try harder; words of affirmation and encouragement or critical words?

> *The best thing my mother-in-law ever did for me was give me words of encouragement especially as far as raising my son was concerned.*
> *—Anonymous*

Respect Your Children's Wishes Concerning Their Children

Kim's daughter-in-law was very particular about avoiding red dye in her son's food. So one thing that Kim always did before feeding her grandson when he was at her house was to look carefully at the label and check to make sure that nothing she was feeding him contained the offending red food dye. One day I asked Kim how she felt about that and she said, "I feel fine about it. It is important to my daughter-in-law so it is important to me."

Kim is a very wise woman. She may have thought being paranoid about red food dye was the dumbest thing she had ever heard, but I'll never know. She never did tell me her opinion because it didn't matter what Kim thought about food dye. Her daughter-in-law was bothered by it, so Kim respected that.

Your daughter-in-law may have a certain way she wants your grandchild dressed, disciplined, or fed. Perhaps she has particular manners that she wants them to practice. You may think that those requests are a waste of time or are totally ridiculous, but if you love and value your daughter-in-law and want a great relationship with her, you will honor her requests. If those requirements are important to her, they should be important to you for no other reason than to respect her and her position as mommy. It's hard to resist someone who treats you and your words and wishes with high regard. That's the kind of mother-in-law we wanted for ourselves and that's how we want to be for our daughters-in-law.

The best thing my mother-in-law ever did for me was let me parent in my own fashion without ever criticizing me. I'm sure she had her opinions.
—Anonymous

Absolutely No Favorites!

I was shocked when I saw a few minutes of a TV program in which the Kardashian girls were giving their mother a lie detector test to discover whether she still had a crush on a former beau even though she is currently married to Bruce Jenner. What is wrong with that picture? All three of her daughters participated in this little experiment. One of their test questions to make sure the lie detector machine was working properly was, "Is Kim your favorite daughter?" Unabashedly, Chris Jenner said, "Yes!" The other two girls just looked at each other. They must have felt horrible as their mother declared publicly she held a more special place in her heart for their sister than for them. Can you imagine how that influences their attitude toward Kim? Isn't the human reaction to dislike the favored one and begin competing with her for their mother's attention and affections?

Favoritism is hurtful and divisive and there should be no place for it in your life if you want a great relationship with your family members. You may feel closer to one child or grandchild than another from time to time. Perhaps you have more in common or just click with one daughter-in-law more than another. Don't show it and don't ever treat one more favorably than the other. Try to keep gifts, attention, phone calls, kind words, encouragement and fun as equally divided as you possibly can. When giving gifts, you don't have to give each one identical presents, but you should try to give a gift of equal value to each. The motto should be equality, but not necessarily uniformity.

It is understood that sometimes one of your family members may have a much greater need than another. If you help one financially, be of help to the other in a different way. You will need to be creative, thoughtful and prayerful in the whole matter.

This takes work and can seem like splitting hairs, but it does wonders to prevent hurt feelings and the demoralizing of your daughter-in-law or other family members. It is one step toward helping them maintain a good relationship with each other and with you. Having harmony and mutual love and respect in your family is worth the effort it takes to treat everyone the same, even if you are not as naturally drawn to one as you are another.

The Bible is filled with examples of human, sinful people showing favoritism to others and the damage that it caused. As referred to previously, the first recorded incidents of playing favorites is in the beginning of the Bible. Genesis tells us that Isaac preferred his older twin, Esau. Rebekah set her affections on Jacob. That did not go well. Apparently Jacob didn't learn from that horrific experience, even though he had to flee for his life from his brother. Jacob's journey away from his hostile brother ended in their mother's homeland. While there, Jacob met and immediately fell in love with a girl named Rachel. He was so smitten by her that he was willing to work for seven years to earn the right to marry her. Jacob's new father-in-law pulled a fast one on him and tricked him into marrying Rachel's older sister, Leah, instead. The next morning Jacob discovered that the young women had been switched. Don't ask me how that could happen. Jacob ended up contracting himself for seven more years of work for the privilege of marrying his favorite, Rachel. Genesis 29:30 says, "Jacob had marital relations with Rachel as well. He loved Rachel more than Leah, so he worked for Laban for seven more years." (NET) It would be bad enough being one of two wives, but can you imagine the heartache you would suffer if you were the wife less loved? I am sure it was devastating to Leah. Later in the narrative Leah is so desperate for some time with her husband that she trades her sister some special food for the privilege of sleeping with this man who preferred another over her. That sounds like desperation and misery. That's what favoritism does. It divides and destroys.

Jacob then compounded the problems within his family by favoring one of his sons, Joseph, over all of his other sons. (Genesis 37:3 NLT) "Jacob loved Joseph more than any of his other children because Joseph had been born to him in his old age. So one day Jacob had a special gift made for Joseph--a beautiful robe." Jacob was not only insensitive enough to favor one of his sons over the others, but he also gave his chosen one a special gift. What was the result of Jacob's behavior? "When his brothers saw that their father loved him more than any of them, they hated him and could not speak a kind word to him. (Genesis 37:4) Those jealous brothers eventually tried to kill Joseph. His oldest brother rescued him, sort of, by selling him into slavery. Through the providence of God, Joseph ended up as a ruler in Egypt where he was eventually able to save his family, the very people who had been cruel to him, from starvation. Only God can pull that off.

There are many more biblical examples of the negative results of showing favoritism, but I think you get the idea. Perhaps it is best to let God's opinion speak for itself.

> "For the LORD your God is God of gods and Lord of lords, the great God, mighty and awesome, who shows no partiality and accepts no bribes." (Deuteronomy 10:17)
>
> "I see very clearly that God shows no favoritism." (Acts 10:34 NLT)
>
> "There is neither Jew nor Greek, slave nor free, male or female, for you are all one in Christ Jesus." (Galatians 3:28)
>
> "My dear brothers and sisters, how can you claim to have faith in our Lord Jesus Christ if you favor some people over others?" (James 2:1 NLT)
>
> "But if you favor some people over others, you are committing a sin. You are guilty of breaking the law." (James 2:9 NLT)

God's word makes very clear that we are to treat everyone as equally as we humanly can. This is not something that we can do on our own. It will take the help, strength and discernment of God as we strive to be the best mothers-in-law and grandmothers that we can be.

My mother-in-law always welcomes our family warmly into her home. She loves having us, no matter how rowdy the kids become. The saying "the more the merrier" was always on her lips – this included having cousins stay over as well. One of her mottos was, "We always have more floor space."
—Anonymous

Minimize Positive Cross-talking

What is cross-talking? I'll give you an example. I witnessed an interaction one day between a friend of mine and her daughter that taught me a lesson to apply to my life as a mother-in-law. My friend Jan has two girls, Shari and Makayla, and each of them has two children. Jan is a devoted mother and grandmother and is very close to both of her girls. She was clueless about one bad habit, however. Whenever Jan was with Shari, she talked about Makayla and Makayla's children. When she was with Makayla, she related stories of Shari and her children. Jan was totally innocent in what she was doing. She was thinking that she was keeping the girls current on each other's lives by sharing stories about the other's children. As she observed Shari's children do something, she would relate to Shari a story of something similar Makayla's children had done.

The problem was that Shari and Makayla were not receiving these anecdotes the way that their mother had intended them. Every time they heard Jan tell a story about the other set of grandkids it seemed like they were being compared. Each felt as though their children were not measuring up. Why couldn't their mother just concentrate on their kids while she was with them?

One day while I was visiting Jan and Shari, she naively relayed another story about Makayla's children to Shari. Shari couldn't take it any longer and looked at her mother and said with a raised voice, "I don't want to hear anything about Makayla's kids again!" Jan was surprised and quickly clamped her mouth closed. I filed that incident away in my brain folder marked, "What Not to Do as a Mother-in-law." From that point on I decided that I would minimize talking about one sibling, in-law or grandchild, even positively, while I am with another. I was going to give my full attention to the family with whom I was spending time.

Think about something similar that has happened to you and how you felt inwardly. While at work your boss tells you what a great job someone else did on a project that both of you worked on, your first thoughts would be to wonder what you did wrong. Why wasn't he also saying great things about you? He may have merely been trying to be complimentary of the other person, but that is not how you heard it. It felt like comparison and it felt as though the other person was superior to you. Or, you have to be gone for a few days to help your parents, and your neighbors graciously invite your husband to come one evening for dinner. When you get home, he raves about how great the meal was and that he had no idea what an incredible cook your neighbor is. It is one of the best meals he has ever had. OK. I went one illustration too far! That not only feels like you are being compared and are coming up short, but it also feels like your husband is a blockhead. You know in your heart that he isn't. He was innocently sharing what happened while you were gone, but that's not how it felt. You are tracking with me, aren't you?

The same thing happens to an even greater degree in families. If your mother-in-law just mentioned in passing how well behaved your sister-in-law's child is, wouldn't your first thought be, "And mine's not? What's wrong with the way my child behaves? She must not think that my little Susie obeys very well or she wouldn't have mentioned it." Hearing compliments about another automatically sets up a situation for comparison.

Why not instead compliment the daughter-in-law and the grandchildren that you are with at the moment? Why say anything that may cause feelings of inadequacy or failure? This does not mean that you never mention the other families or the other grandchildren, but simply minimize the discussion of them. Enjoy the ones you are with.

My mother-in-law treats me like I am the most wonderful person she knows (she treats all of her daughters-in-law like this). She has only uplifting and encouraging words to say to my family. She lives for Christ with such humility and treats others with compassion, living out Philippians 2:3-8. Plus, she thinks I look waaaay younger than I am. I love her and want to be like her when I grow up.
—Anonymous

Eliminate Negative Cross-talking

It goes without saying (or maybe it needs to be said) that you should never talk disparagingly about one family member to another.

Many who would not think of speaking badly about someone outside of their family can be cruel to people to whom they are related. Gossip is gossip, whether it is outside or inside the family, and in every case it is deplorable to God. It always tears down rather than builds up. Listen to what the Bible says about gossip.

> "Let no corrupting talk come out of your mouths, but only such as is good for building up, as fits the occasion, that it may give grace to those who hear." (Ephesians 4:29 ESV)

> "Keep your tongue from evil and your lips from speaking deceit." (Psalm 34:13 ESV)

> "If anyone thinks he is religious and does not bridle his tongue but deceives his heart, *this person's religion is worthless*." (James 1:26 ESV) (emphasis added)

I know that you don't want your family members to think your religion is worthless. Therefore, there is no room for speaking poorly to your daughter-in-law about any member of your family. It will sow seeds of hard feelings and distrust and will be counterproductive to building a good relationship with her. It will also make her wonder what you say about her when she is not around. She will conclude that if you talk *to her* about someone, you will also talk *about her* to others.

You can control what you say to your daughter-in-law, but it is harder when your daughter-in-law speaks derogatorily or gossips about another family member to you. You can't be a willing participant in that either because the same principles hold true. Gossip is abhorrent to God and it erodes the foundation of trust between two people. If she talks about others, she will talk about you. Never think that the rumormonger, even if she is your daughter-in-law, will hold a confidence or that you are exempt from her tongue because you are special. People act consistently with their character.

So what do you do? As the mother-in-law you are in a very precarious position. One way of dealing with slanderous talk is to say to your daughter-in-law, "Oh my goodness! Let's stop and pray for that person right now!" That is not the payoff a gossip wants from their "sharing." Then do it and mean it. If that doesn't work, an even more direct approach is required. You can simply say, "I just can't listen to that." This is another perfect time to send up an arrow prayer and ask God to guide you as you navigate your way through these murky waters. Yes, you want to have a good relationship with your daughter-in-law, but not at the cost of your character. What looks and feels like a "good" relationship may just be a flimsy, empty "going along to get along" relationship. You may live a pseudo-peaceful existence, at least when you are face to face, but she will have no respect for you or your faith. *Your religion will be worthless.* (James 1:26b)

Who would have thought that being a mother-in-law would have such an impact on grand-parenting? It is a joy when those little ones come along, and that experience is made even more wonderful when there is a friendly, cooperative spirit between the two sets of grandparents and love and consideration for the rest of the family members involved.

The best thing my mother-in-law ever did for me (other than give me her son!!), was tell me that I'm a good mom. I needed to hear it from her, and it was a blessing when she said it.
—Anonymous

Chapter 7

Over the Long Haul

Improving Your Relationship Through the Years

> "Instead, be kind to each other, tenderhearted, forgiving one another, just as God through Christ has forgiven you."
> (Ephesians 4:32 NLT 2007)

"Dear Abby" is a syndicated advice column that has been published in newspapers throughout the United States for the last fifty years. A recurring topic that threads throughout the thousands of letters that have been submitted over the decades has to do with the strained relationships between mothers-in-law and daughters-in-law. This tension is a source of grief for both.

An example of one young wife's heartache was printed in the "Dear Abby" column on October 22, 2012. This wife wrote that when she first married her husband, she was sure she had a great mother-in-law. "Boy was I wrong. Now, five years later, I can't stand her. Just 15 minutes with her sends me over the edge. She's rude, judgmental, and gossips like a teenager about everyone." In the letter, she confides that her mother-in-law actually fessed up to purposely leaving important ingredients out of recipes she shared with her daughter-in-law so that her son would prefer his mother's cooking over his wife's.

Her mother-in-law's actions would be hurtful by anyone's standards. The young daughter-in-law was so desperate for a solution to her mother-in-law problem that she wrote a letter to a newspaper advice column to get help.

Obviously, this mother-in-law had no intention of having a good relationship with her daughter-in-law. In fact, there was little thought of her daughter-in-law at all. Mama's entire focus was self-centered and selfish. Her goal was to gain favor with her son, but everything she was doing was destroying the very thing that she wanted to accomplish. She was so blinded by her egocentric desires that she was sabotaging her own goals. The only good news in this story was that her son was on his wife's side "100 percent" when it came to his mother. The bad news; her daughter-in-law "can't stand her" and her beloved son was "ready to pack in Ohio." The situation was so repugnant, they actually were considering a move to get away from his mother.

One of the most important keys to a successful relationship with your married children is, *cultivate a great relationship with your daughter-in-law and that will naturally lead to having a meaningful connection to your son*. Chances are you already are in good relationship with your son. You don't need to do anything more to win him over. If you try to damage his wife's reputation or usurp her position as the most important female in his life, you can only lose ground in the bond with your son. Your actions toward his wife are communicating nonverbally to him what you believe about his choices and judgment. After all, he chose her. If you value her and do all you can to have a bond with your daughter-in-law, you are valuing and validating his choice. If you have a poor relationship with your son, undermining his selection in a wife is not going to do anything to improve it.

So, mother-in-law, how can you accomplish building a growing rapport with your daughter-in-law through the years? Surely after you have been a mother-in-law for a while, there is nothing else that you can do to cause your relationship with your daughter-in-law to flourish! Oh, but there is!

I am not sure I can name just one but, the best thing my mother-in-law ever did for me was to raise such a strong man of God, [she] consistently prays for me, [and did] even before she knew me, and then after being welcomed into the family she has never treated me as anything less than a daughter!
—Anonymous

Mother-in-law Be-attitudes

She has been your daughter-in-law for a few years now and you have either fallen into a comfortable pattern in how you relate to one another or you are embroiled in a cold or hot war. She is likely a mommy and hopefully you are a happy grandmother. It would be so easy just to let things flow along rather than putting forth the effort that it takes to continue to try to build closeness, understanding and a deep friendship. There are a few things that you can do that will make the results well worth the energy.

Be Trustworthy - Keep a Confidence

"Ready to Pack in Ohio" could not trust her mother-in-law with any information because she "gossiped like a teenager about everyone." *Be* the kind of person that your daughter-in-law can confide in and know for certain that the confidence will never be broken. A person of character is one who can hold a secret. It is much easier to build a relationship with someone who has the self-concept and the will-power not to share with others things that have been conveyed to them. And, mother-in-law, your daughter-in-law gets to be the person to determine what will be told and what will not. If she shares something with you and asks you not to tell, you don't get to go home and weigh its "secret" value, determine it's not that big a deal and then pass it on. Your mouth must be like a steel trap that will not open under penalty of law.

Your daughter-in-law is like any friend that is trying to establish trust. She may divulge a small tidbit to you at first to see if it will come back to her. Trust has to be gained over time. The more she sees you are trustworthy, the more she will have confidence to share. Once you break that trust, it is very difficult to regain it. It may take more years than you have.

Dr. Gary Smalley has an excellent word picture in his book *Love is a Decision*, concerning a person whose spirit has been wounded, which is what our betrayal of trust does to our daughters-in-law. He describes our spirits as though we are an open hand. When someone comes and jabs us or hurts us, our spirit closes up just as our hand would if it were poked. It takes a long time to open our spirits again to that hurtful person just as it does to establish trust in the one who has betrayed us.

Don't do it. Don't have loose lips. *Be* a person who can hold a confidence. There are two exceptions to this rule. The first concerns your husband. It is not a good policy in any marriage to make agreements to keep secrets from one another. When your daughter-in-law or anyone tells you something and asks you not to tell anyone else, tell them before they share that you would like to reserve the right to talk to your husband about it. That is, of course, if he is trustworthy which I assume he is or you wouldn't be married to him. Go on to explain that you don't ever promise to intentionally keep anything from him. It is not a given that you will talk to him about whatever she is about to tell you (my husband is not into hearing about OB/GYN problems or girly type things), but don't promise that you won't. Fortunately this works for us because my husband has proven himself to be a man of honor and if he is not supposed to tell something, you can't pry his jaws open with a crow bar. Try to make this position clear with your daughter-in-law's full knowledge before the confidence is shared.

The only other time something private can be shared is if there is a crime being committed or there is genuine harm being done to the person who is sharing. You cannot stand by and watch someone harmed. Go to the proper authorities as quickly as possible.

Something I really appreciate about my mother-in-law is she makes a killer pie and she taught me how! She also raised a great son, and gave me advice for my two [sons]! I hope my daughters-in-law feel the same.
—*Anonymous*

Be Timely

If you tell your daughter-in-law that you are going to be someplace at a certain time, do everything within your power to be there. Your daughter-in-law will determine if she can trust you to be where you said you were going to be when you said you would be there if you are punctual. Of course, anyone can have something unexpectedly delay them, but is your habit that of being timely? Or, is your reputation like Mrs. Slowsky, the tortoise on the popular high speed internet commercial? If you are routinely late and don't meet with your daughter-in-law when you say you will, you are telegraphing two things. The first is that the person you were just with or the situation you were just in is more important and holds more value to you than the person or situation to which you are going (in this case, her). Is that the message that you want to give her? Do you really want her to believe that other things and other people rank above her?

The second message persistent tardiness is conveying is that you are not trustworthy as far as time management is concerned. She simply cannot be sure that you will arrive when you say you will and that erodes her trust level in you and in your word. Make it your aim to be a timely person.

If you have already disappointed your daughter-in-law in this area, there are some things you can do. Go to her and tell her you are sorry that she hasn't been able to count on you to be on time. Tell her that you don't want her to think that other things are more important than her. Ask her for her help to keep you accountable by calling you on it whenever you are late. Then pray, ask for God's help to judge your time better, begin starting out sooner and if need be, set your clock ahead. Talk to others who have conquered the "late monster" and see how they have achieved success.

Keep in mind; if constantly being late wears away your daughter-in-law's trust in you, it is eating away others confidence in you as well. Try your best with God's help to make every effort to be on time.

> *The best thing my mother-in-law ever did for me was allow us to move in with her for three years when we had nowhere else to go.*
> —Anonymous

Be a Promise Keeper

Connie is a delightful lady who is generous and fun to be around. Her problem is that she commits to things and then doesn't follow through with them. Connie will make a lunch date and cancel at the last minute. She agrees to watch her grandchildren and if the least little thing comes up or she just doesn't feel like it, she cancels. She will plan activities at church and not follow through. In fact, this backing out of things at the last minute has become such a normal part of Connie's life and reputation that everyone calls her Cancelling Connie behind her back. It has become a joke and people smile whenever Connie agrees to do something because one just never knows if it will really happen. The activity that she commits to might get done but chances are just as good that it might not. It has evolved to the place that when Connie plans an activity or agrees to do something, the parishioners pencil it onto their calendar so that it can be easily erased. Connie is a lovely Christian woman, but she has never made the mental connection between her actions and the fact that people don't trust her to keep her word.

It has been said that it is better to be consistently bad than inconsistent because at least when we are consistently bad those around us know what to expect. I am not encouraging anyone to be a consistently bad mother-in-law, but I do want to persuade all mothers-in-law to keep their word. If you agree to do something with or for your daughter-in-law, try everything within your power to follow through on that commitment. Do what you said you would do without any strings attached. Do it because you said it and that's how a person of integrity responds.

If you consistently follow through and keep your promises, your daughter-in-law will know that you can be trusted. In a world of distrust and broken pledges, you can be one person on whom she can truly depend. *Be* one who keeps your word and that will go a long way in building your relationship with your daughter-in-law.

The best thing my mother-in-law ever did for me was take care of the grandbabies so mom and dad could have some alone time.
—Anonymous

Be a Listener

There are not many things that say "love" more than someone giving you the gift of really hearing you; not just your words but your heart. *Knowing that you are heard* can validate you as a person and validate your feelings. It draws you closer to the one who listens and enhances your relationship.

On the other hand, hardly anything can make you feel as invisible as the experience of speaking and having someone ignore you, discount or trivialize what you say, or talk right over you as if you weren't talking. If your intent is to have a good relationship with your daughter-in-law, you don't want to be counted among the ones who don't really listen.

There are some tricks to listening to your daughter-in-law that can be helpful in causing you to draw closer to her. You probably discovered when your son was a teenager that you can't force a blissful time of sharing. The same is true in other relationships. I wish it could be up to you to decide the moment when you are going to have a deep, meaningful, life-changing conversation with your daughter-in-law. Unfortunately, you can't count on that happening. What you can decide to do, however, is be available to listen when she is ready to talk. When that moment comes, drop whatever you are doing and *hear her out!* May I add that it will very likely be at a time that is inconvenient for you? Don't let that sidetrack you. If at all possible, stop what you are doing and listen.

This is an area in which I have been deficient. I went to a ladies' retreat several years ago and felt as though it was a total waste of time. I thought the speaker was boring, the food was marginal and it just wasn't any fun. But, there was one thing that kept bubbling to the surface of my mind every time I thought of that blah retreat. That boring speaker had the nerve to say, "Let God interrupt your agenda." Ow! Did she realize what she was saying? Did she have any idea how many commitments I have each day? My agenda is sacred. I awaken every morning with my list knowing exactly what I need to accomplish and she wants me to let it be interrupted? Then I realized that, no, she didn't know or care about any of those things. Actually it was God that wanted me to be flexible to His plan for me each day. That one truth from that retreat made it well worth the time and money spent to be there. By the grace of God, I started looking for Him more in my day to see where He would want to use me. I began to learn that He wanted me tuned into people more than my "to do" list. I tried to be more available to God, but old habits die hard. I didn't realize quite how hard until the day that I referred to in the previous chapter when Nicole told me I always seemed to be in a hurry to get off of the phone! Even though it wasn't something I was consciously doing, I knew she was right. I realized that she was never going to open up and really talk to me if I was consistently in a hurry to move on with my list. The risk of her being shut down, rejected, or brushed off was just too great. There is nothing on my agenda that is more important to me than having a great relationship with my daughters-in-law. I am so grateful to her for being brave enough to tell me that. I try to be more tuned into my daughters-in-law now. I'm not always successful, but I'm making an effort to mentally drop the thing that is screaming for my attention so that when *they are ready* to talk, they have my full focus. What I learned almost too late was that if I continue to brush them off, even unknowingly, they will quit telling me anything. If I lose the opportunity to hear them, I lose the chance to validate them and grow to be their friend as much as their mother-in-law.

Stopping everything to listen will be a bit more difficult for some than others. I have been made aware that people usually fall into one of two categories. Either they lean more toward being task-oriented or their predisposition is to be relationship-oriented. The story of two of Jesus' best friends in the Bible, Mary and Martha perfectly illustrate the difference. Luke 10:38-42 says, "As Jesus and his disciples were on their way, he came to a village where a woman named Martha opened her home to him. She had a sister called Mary, who sat at the Lord's feet listening to what he said. But Martha was distracted by all the preparations that had to be made. She came to him and asked, 'Lord, don't you care that my sister has left me to do the work by myself? Tell her to help me!' 'Martha, Martha,' the Lord answered, 'you are worried and upset about many things, but few things are needed—or indeed only one. *Mary has chosen what is better*, and it will not be taken away from her.'" (Emphasis added) Jesus loved them both, but He let Martha know that concentrating on her relationship with Him was more important than making sure the house was clean and everything was in the proper order. Touché.

I'm sure that you have heard the axiom that says, when it is time to die, you won't regret not having worked more or cleaned your home more, but you could regret not having spent real time loving, listening and being in authentic relationship with your family. If you are a "Martha" and tasks are always calling you, pledge with God's help that you will be more in tune to your daughter-in-law and the next time she talks, you will listen. Vow to be a "Mary" and "choose what is better."

Not only do you need to be ready to listen when your daughter-in-law is ready to talk, but you need to show you are listening. By engaging your whole body, you communicate to her that what she is saying to you at that moment is as important to you as it is to her. First, you must stop what you are doing. Put down the wooden spoon, drop your needlework, close the book and turn off the television. Turn your body toward her and look at your daughter-in-law. Her demeanor and body language will tell you a lot about her emotion as she begins to speak to you. If she has a big smile that is about to consume her entire face and her hand is resting protectively on her stomach, you may be on the verge of getting some exciting news. If you are preoccupied doing another task while she is trying to share this life-changing information, you are diminishing her and at risk of missing out on sharing the excitement of this experience.

Perhaps you look at your daughter-in-law and see that her eyes are red and puffy, her head is down and her shoulders are slumped, you know that her heart is heavy and you can be praying before she even begins to tell you what is on her mind.

Once again, you have to be looking at her and not multitasking so you can get a clue as to what is happening. Looking at your daughter-in-law will enable you to "read" her which will help you know how to respond appropriately.

Another key to listening that conveys that you truly "hear," rests in the emotional posture that you take. No matter what your daughter-in-law tells you, don't be defensive. Try not to wear your feelings on your sleeve or constantly make excuses. If you always have your defenses up, you will prohibit your daughter-in-law from telling you how she really feels about things. It is akin to trying to switch on the lamp every evening only to get a shock. It won't be long before you throw away that lamp. I am not implying that there won't be times when you need to give a defense of something that you have done or that you shouldn't ever feel defensive. What I am saying is don't bear an ongoing defensive demeanor. That will be a show stopper and it will end your opportunity to listen.

Finally, have you ever shared an insight or something that was meaningful to you only to have the person with whom you shared it look at you with a blank expression? It is obvious that person is not in sync with you or resonating with you in any way. It can make you wonder why you shared something that precious with them in the first place. One way that you can avoid that same experience with your daughter-in-law is to be engaged in the conversation and mirror her emotion. Be excited about the things she is excited about. Show an interest in the things in which she is interested. Relate to her as much as you can. It is far easier to share with someone with whom you can identify. The purpose is not to be a fake but to be a true friend. To have a daughter-in-law who is a friend is a blessing that defies words and conventional wisdom. That friendship can only come about by truly listening to her and hearing her heart.

All of these techniques of listening are to help you to show your daughter-in-law that you value her and you respect what she has to say. The mother-in-law listening motto is: stop, look and listen. If you do those things, your daughter-in-law will trust you and talk to you and you will be on the road to having her as a real friend.

My mother-in-law is beautiful inside and out. She gives the best advice and sometimes just an ear. She has always made me feel part of the family.
—Anonymous

Be a Grace Giver

Mercy and grace have to be two of the most beautiful words in the English language. Mercy has been defined as *not* giving someone what they *do* deserve and grace as giving someone what they *don't* deserve. Both of these words are characterized by Jesus. He does *not* give the one who puts her trust in Him the punishment she deserves for her sin. What He does instead is give her friendship with Him and eternal life which she doesn't deserve.

There are opportunities within all relationships to be a grace giver, but perhaps none more than in the mother-in-law/daughter-in-law relationship. If this gift of God's grace is so incredible when extended to us, can you imagine how wonderful your daughter-in-law feels when you offer grace to her, especially when she doesn't deserve it? But, how do you do that?

Judy was impressed by her son's beautiful, accomplished new wife, Stephanie. She was on a government assignment when she and Judy's son, Conor met. After a whirlwind courtship, they were married. It wasn't long after the wedding that Judy began to notice some behavior that concerned her. On occasion, Stephanie exhibited very controlling behavior punctuated by bursts of anger for what seemed to be trivial reasons. Things weren't always awkward, but certain situations were so unsettling that there were definitely red flags. Despite her unease, Judy was determined to be a great mother-in-law. Stephanie and Conor seemed to be holding it together through the ups and downs.

Judy was delighted that she didn't have to wait long for her first grandbaby. She rushed out and bought her new little grandson a tricycle and excitedly took it to Conor and Stephanie's to give to the baby. Stephanie opened the beautifully wrapped gift. When she saw what it was she said, "He doesn't need that. We're taking it back." Stephanie did just that and kept the money for herself.

Judy was so hurt and disappointed that she didn't know how to respond. She went home and cried and prayed and asked God how she was ever going to have a good relationship with someone that was so volatile and thoughtless. Gradually God brought peace to Judy's heart and gave her a plan. She became a student of Stephanie and learned about her life growing up as well as her extended family and background. Judy knew that Stephanie's dad had been a pastor, but what she didn't know was that he could be a cruel man. He preached one thing while at church, but outside of church he lived another. Judy discovered that when Stephanie was younger and their family played games together, her father would become so competitive and angry that he would actually hit Stephanie with his fist. Judy came to the realization that Stephanie entered into her marriage with Conor a terribly wounded person. She decided that her course of action was that she was going to be a grace giver. She was going to give Stephanie what her actions didn't deserve. Judy started thinking of Stephanie as a little wounded animal and approached her as one would approach the wounded. She didn't rush in on Stephanie emotionally nor demand apologies when Stephanie acted out. Instead, she would visit their home and just sit with Stephanie, she would love her without strings attached and with no judgment until Stephanie could see that Judy could be trusted. Judy said the most difficult thing through the whole process was waiting for years and years, loving and trusting God until Stephanie could see that Judy was going to love her no matter what she did. Judy made the decision to love and be a grace giver and God helped her with the rest.

What your daughter-in-law wants more than anything is to be loved and accepted with her flaws, mistakes, and even with her occasional thoughtlessness, or rudeness. You would like the same thing from her, wouldn't you? As a mother-in-law it is likely that you have at least twenty to thirty years of age and experience on your daughter-in-law, so give her a break. Understand that she is in the process of maturing and growing as you still are. You just happen to be a little farther down the road than she is. She is going to make mistakes and perhaps even offend you from time to time, but try to remember how you wanted your mother-in-law to treat you. Also consider the great gift of grace that you have been given by God.

Besides loving unconditionally is there anything else that you can do to help you be a grace giver? Following, you will find two more things that can be practiced in order to be a mother-in-law that gives grace to her daughter-in-law.

My mother-in-law encouraged me in my parenting and in my life as a wife. She showed true concern and care for each one of our lives.
—*Anonymous*

Be Forgiving

Forgiveness is a choice, not a feeling. It is a loving, voluntary cancellation of debt, pardon or letting go. When you forgive someone, you are releasing your right for payback or retribution and are leaving that up to God. And, I might add, it is a totally unnatural act.

Judy had the option of going away from her daughter-in-law's rude behavior with an unforgiving attitude that could have lasted for the rest of her life. She could have demanded an apology or refused to speak to Stephanie. She could have remembered this transgression and brought it up every time she had the opportunity. Those actions were all choices that she could make. But, those actions would have produced the exact opposite result of what Judy was trying to accomplish within her relationship with her daughter-in-law, and within her own spirit.

Forgiveness requires a lot of us. There is nothing human or normal about it. Forgiveness causes us to set aside our selfishness and not demand what we think is our due. Injustices remain and wounds still cause pain, but with God's help we can forgive. Many times we have to go to God again and again giving Him the dregs of what we thought we had committed to Him long ago. If we persist in the process, He will bring us genuine freedom.

If forgiveness is so difficult and counter to every human inclination that you have, why do you need to forgive your daughter-in-law or anyone for that matter? The first reason is because you have been forgiven so much. To illustrate that point, Jesus tells a parable in Matthew 18 about a man that owed a tremendous debt. In today's dollars it would be more than our national debt. The man was thrown into prison until he could pay that crushing amount. First, it's more than any person could ever accumulate and second, how could he get money to pay back a debt if he was in prison? Jesus purposely used that word picture to show us the total helplessness of the man who owed the debt. The benevolent king had mercy on the man, however, and not only released him from prison but forgave the huge amount of money the man owed. That forgiven person turned around and went out to find a man that owed him 100 days wages. Instead of showing the same forgiving attitude, he physically assaulted him and demanded his money. The man who owed the smaller debt begged for mercy to no avail. The forgiven man had the one indebted to him thrown into prison. He should have had a grateful heart and attitude because of the underserved forgiveness that he received. Instead, his unmerciful actions toward his fellow man were an insult to the king who had forgiven him. When we fail to forgive, it is an insult to the One who has forgiven us so much.

If that is not compelling enough, there is another reason we should forgive. God has commanded us to. At the beginning of this chapter is the verse, Ephesians 4:32. It says, "Be kind and compassionate to one another, *forgiving each other*, just as in Christ God forgave you." (Emphasis added) Colossians 3:13 also says, "Bear with each other and *forgive whatever grievances you may have against one another*. Forgive as the Lord forgave you." (NIV 1978) (emphasis added) Refusing to forgive others is an act of direct disobedience against God. Disobedience equals sin. Unconfessed sin ruins the sweetness of our fellowship with God and it robs us of our joy. As Christians we should be obsessed with forgiveness and not vengeance.

Un-forgiveness also chains us to the past. It lets another control our emotions. "She" makes me mad. "She" hurt me. "She" determines if I am going to that family function or not. We never freely move past that moment when we were offended. We are constantly reminded of it and that tethers us to it. It is bondage and not what Christ wants for us. He came to set us free. Forgiveness is the road to freedom.

Another powerful reason to forgive is that un-forgiveness becomes a toxin. It poisons the heart and mind with bitterness distorting one's whole perspective on life. It can spread to family and friends and it can kill reputations and relationships.

Finally, we must forgive if we want to be forgiven. In the Lord's Prayer Jesus said, "Forgive us our debts as we forgive our debtors." (Matthew 6:12) That is the only verse in the Lord's Prayer that Jesus elaborated on. He went on to say in Matthew 6:14 and 15, "For if you forgive men when they sin against you, your heavenly Father will also forgive you. *But if you do no forgive men their sins, your Father will not forgive your sins."* (emphasis added) That's a sobering thought. What if God forgave our debts only in the measure and in the same time frame that it takes us to forgive others?

According to everything that I have studied, this verse is not directed to the person who is having difficulty forgiving or is in the process of forgiving. Fortunately, God's grace is applied to us when we will to forgive and are working toward it. This verse is for the person who has a *disposition of un-forgiveness*. They are the ones who dig in their heels and say, "I will *not* forgive." I sat at a lady's kitchen table one day when she told me a story of a bad experience that she had with one of her in-laws. She flatly stated that she "would never forgive that person as long as she lived." As far as I know, she never did and she died a dried up, lonely, embittered old woman. The only thing harder than forgiving is the opposite; not forgiving.

Speaker and author, Beth Moore says that we are never more like God than when we forgive. He forgives all who come to Him despite the crime, but He doesn't stop there. He turns lives around and uses them for good. Just look to the scriptures and see Abraham the liar, Jacob the deceiver, Moses the murderer, David the adulterer, Matthew the cheat, Paul the bully and Mary Magdelyn the prostitute. He can turn your life around just as dramatically if you come to Him for forgiveness and then have a forgiving spirit toward others.

You now know why you should forgive and what happens when there is a failure to forgive, but did you know there are other fringe benefits of forgiving? The first is that forgiveness halts the cycle of blame. Have you seen the devise in malls that have a slot in the top in which a coin can be dropped? The coin then circles around and around until it finally falls in the hole in the center. I become mesmerized when I watch that coin orbit so many times. That's how the blame game goes. Accusations of fault circle between you and your daughter-in-law affecting everyone who comes near and gets sucked up in the tornado of words. Resentment is what happens if the cycle goes uninterrupted. Every time you remember, every time you go to that bitter place in your mind, every time you relive that incident, you are "feeling" it again. Resentment clings to the past, relives it and picks over the fresh scab so that the wound never heals. Be the one to break the cycle. Forgive.

Another benefit of forgiveness is that it gives freedom. Lewis Smedes, renowned Christian author, ethicist and theologian points out, "The first and often the only person to be healed by forgiveness is the person who does the forgiving. When we genuinely forgive, we set the prisoner free and discover that the prisoner we set free was us." There is wonderful, liberating freedom when we forgive. We are free from the sin of unforgiveness. We are free from being imprisoned in the past. We are free from the poison or toxin that erodes our character, our demeanor and our faith. We are free from someone else controlling us. Freedom is worth it.

Finally, forgiveness thwarts Satan. Paul urged the Corinthians in 2 Corinthians 2:11 to forgive "so that no advantage be taken of us by Satan, for we are not ignorant of his schemes." (NASB) To refuse to forgive is to fall into Satan's trap. However, his entire scheme is undermined when we forgive. It is very hard to divide a family full of forgiving people. It is difficult to permanently sever the relationship between a mother-in-law and her daughter-in-law when they have forgiving spirits. Having a continuing disposition of forgiveness ruins Satan's plans and that's a great reason to forgive.

But now we are down to the nitty-gritty. How do we do it? The only way that we can truly forgive "from the heart" is with the help and grace of God. If you are struggling with forgiving your daughter-in-law for something that she has said or done, first make the choice to forgive, then, tell Jesus how you feel about what she did. You can be honest with Him. He knows it anyway. Ask Him to change your heart and attitude. Then, even though you don't *feel* forgiving, *will* to forgive. The deliberate choice that you make to forgive will almost always run contrary to your feelings. Refuse to hold a grudge, resist the temptation to retaliate, refuse bitterness and reject brooding. Ask God to help you to release your daughter-in-law from your judgment. With God's help you can do it.

Judy was hurt and offended by the callous way her daughter-in-law treated her. She willed to forgive because of her relationship with Jesus and because she valued having a great relationship with her daughter-in-law. She broke the cycle of unforgiveness before it could get a vise grip on her. Now she is free to really love her daughter-in-law. Everything is not all bliss. She continues to get hurt from time to time, but she also continues to choose forgiveness.

One of the best things my mother-in-law ever did for me was she gave me recipes of my husband's favorite foods.
—Anonymous

Be Hard to Offend

One day I ran into a lady that I knew from church that I had not seen in a while. I told her that I had missed seeing her at church. She told me emphatically that she was not coming back. Then she relayed her story of the crime that had been committed against her the last time she attended. She had been sitting in Sunday School one day when a young mother came in carrying her baby. While trying to move past this lady into the row, the young mom bumped her with the baby's diaper bag and "didn't even say she was sorry." I honestly cannot remember how I responded that day, but even now my thoughts are, "you have *got* to be kidding me!" Now *I* was starting to get offended. Didn't this lady realize that it was a major triumph that this poor momma even made it to church with a baby in tow? I'm sure the young mother had her purse on one arm and a diaper bag on the other, all while holding the baby and struggling to get past everyone in the row so that she could finally sit down. Furthermore, I doubt if she had any idea that her diaper bag even touched the insulted woman. Talk about being easily offended! Proverbs 19:11 says, "A person's wisdom yields patience; it is to one's glory to overlook an offense."

Don't look for things to offend you in your relationship with your daughter-in-law. If you look hard enough, you can always find something. Don't be supersensitive and try not to have thin skin. Instead, always be looking for reasons to give your daughter-in-law a break. When she has said something that has been offensive or has hurt your feelings, try to feel what she was feeling at that moment and put yourself in her shoes. Seek to get understanding why she popped off as she did. Remember back to your early years of marriage, motherhood and the pressures and insecurities that you felt periodically. Reframing the situation will help you to see things through your daughter-in-law's eyes and will go a long way to helping you "overlook an offense."

If there is an issue that really needs to be dealt with, go to your daughter-in-law and talk to her about it. If she was just having a bad day or her hormones were the ones doing the talking, let it pass. My mother always said, "If it is worth a war, have a war, but if it is not worth a war, (which is most often the case) don't have a war!" Your relationship with your daughter-in-law will go much more smoothly if you are always looking for the best in her and you are hard to offend.

> *One thing I really appreciated about my mother-in-law was that she didn't ever try to tell me how to raise my kids or feed my husband. She just assumed I knew what I was doing on both fronts, even when sometimes I really didn't.*
> —Anonymous

Be One Who Preaches With Your Life, Not With Your Mouth

It was an interesting and exciting Sunday when a Messianic Jew came to our church to speak about how he had come to personal faith in Jesus as his Messiah. He shared about the thrill and fulfillment that he experienced as a result of his new found faith. He was so excited at the beginning of his Christian/Jewish life that he desperately wanted all of his family to know the same joy that he did. His problem was that he was overbearing and thought that he could coerce, nag and bully his family into believing in Jesus as Messiah, whether they wanted to or not. He told of being so enthusiastic about his new life that he resorted to putting gospel tracts into their boxes of cereal so that when they poured the cereal into their bowl in the morning, out would plop a little pamphlet telling them why they needed Jesus. Hopefully, he was joking about that part. In fact, all of his "in your face" attempts to share Jesus only served to annoy them, as it would me, especially if I had not had my coffee.

Mothers-in-law do the same thing. Understandably, if your adult children don't know Jesus personally, the inclination is to panic. You are willing to do about anything to get them to "see the light." You give them Bible verses, you spiritualize everything, and you talk church or Bible study until you are blue in the face. Maybe some of you have even tried the Bible tracts in their cereal box technique.

The best thing you can do, however, is pray for them and then live an authentic Christian life in front of them. If your grown children were raised going to church and know the way to Jesus, there is nothing new that you can tell them. They have heard it all. Continuing to harp at them, no matter how well-intentioned, is not going to accomplish anything but drive them away. If you came to faith later in life and your adult kids don't know about Jesus, just live your faith in front of them at first. Hopefully they will notice the change for the better in your conduct and they just may ask you what has happened. If they don't, after praying for God's discernment and guidance, ask them if you can tell them something incredible that's happened to you. If they say yes, consider that an opening from God and happily share the new joy that you are now experiencing because Jesus has forgiven you of your sins and given you a new reason for living. Ask them for forgiveness for not living the way you should have when you were raising them. Be as specific as you can be. If you yelled too much, drank too much, or were uncaring or mean, apologize for those things. Getting permission to tell them about your faith and then approaching your children with a spirit of humility will make them much more open to really listening to you.

If your kids say they don't want to hear about it right now, you have to respect that. They are not yet ready to hear your story. Keep praying for them to be open to God's Spirit speaking to them. Pray for yourself that you will live like a true believer and pray for an opportunity to get to share with them what God has done in your life. Trust God to speak to them in His time. You heard Him and answered His call. He can cause them to hear Him too.

> *The best thing my mother-in-law ever did for me was show me an example of a Christian that eventually led me to finding the Lord.*
> *—Anonymous*

Be Aware that Your Son is Not Perfect

You will never have a great relationship with your daughter-in-law if you think she isn't good enough for your son. You have to get over that, Momma. It's hard to admit that your son is not perfect. Somehow you think that it is a reflection on you or your childrearing skills if your son shows some flaws. If he messes up, that means you did something wrong or you were a bad mom, doesn't it? No, not necessarily. He is an adult and can make his own life choices. Our tendency as mothers is to take too much credit when our kids do well and too much blame when they do poorly. The truth is that we do the best we can with God's help and then it is up to them when they become adults.

One day I shared with a friend that I was writing a book about loving your daughter-in-law. She looked at me and said emphatically, "no one is good enough for my son." Her son happens to be married. What did that say about how she feels about her daughter-in-law? That poor girl doesn't have a chance of having a good relationship with my friend, her mother-in-law, because she's already defeated by virtue of being less than perfect. It wasn't that my friend disliked her son's wife. He could be married to anyone and they wouldn't be good enough. Believe me, my friend's son is not perfect, but in her eyes he is, and her daughter-in-law will always come up short.

All three of my daughters-in-law have called me at some point and told me that my sons are slobs. They are tired of the guys leaving their socks on the floor or piles of clothes where they shouldn't. I could get defensive and feel threatened that they think I didn't do a very good job of disciplining or training the boys when they were growing up. The truth is, the girls are right. Those guys can be slobs. So my response is usually, "Yep. They are yours now. I never did succeed in that area and so maybe they will do better for you than they did for me." Often I find myself relating more to the girls than I do my own sons. I try to see their point of view and listen without being defensive or combative when they call to tell me things about the guys. When I do that, they feel more and more freedom to call and talk and I am much more aware of what is really going on in their homes.

Part of having a great relationship is having open and honest communication. If your daughter-in-law tells you something that is less than flattering about your son, forgo your impulse to immediately align with your son. Stop and think. Is she just blowing off steam or does what she is saying have real merit? Don't be defensive. Just listen and try to relate to her.

If what she tells you about your son is said with evil intent, is a lie, slanderous, or said for the purpose of getting even, you may not want to say anything. Pray and think first. Anything you say to her at that moment can and will be held against you. In a situation where you believe your daughter-in-law is emotionally unstable, seek the help of professionals to know how to handle it. Keep in mind as you are reading, this book will be of very little help for a toxic relationship. Those kinds of circumstances are better dealt with by experts who deal with emotional or psychological issues on an ongoing basis.

But back to the run-of-the-mill momma who thinks her son is perfect. It's wonderful that you love your son, but try to look at him objectively. Imagine seeing him through your daughter-in-law's eyes. Remember that all of us are flawed human beings. Romans 3:23 says, "For all have sinned and fall short of the glory of God." When you place your son in the "perfect" category, you are giving him a position that was meant for Jesus alone. There has only been one mom in the history of the world that has had bragging rights to having the perfect son. It's not you and it's not me. Understanding your son for who he truly is, flaws and all will help build a better relationship with your daughter-in-law.

The best thing my mother-in-law ever did for me was she gave me a wonderful, amazing man, husband and soul mate.
—Anonymous

Be Calm in Crisis

Anne's mother-in-law was a Christian, but it would be difficult for an onlooker to tell by how she responded in times of crisis. The woman could come unglued at the least little incident. If she heard there was a car wreck in the town in which Anne lived, she would be convinced that her son and daughter-in-law were among the dead. She would call repeatedly until she was able to speak to them in person and be reassured that they would live to see another day. If Anne allowed one of her children to lie on the floor to watch TV, her mother-in-law would literally grab her chest and have a "spell," all the while proclaiming that those kids were going to join her in the afterlife from catching pneumonia. When a true emergency came along, Anne would not only have to deal with the situation but also with her mother-in-law who managed to plan all of their funerals while she was drifting toward her own death.

I make light of Anne's dilemma, but most of the time it was not funny to Anne. She couldn't understand why her mother-in-law, who said she trusted Jesus, didn't live like she did. Did her mother-in-law truly believe that Jesus sees her and knows what is happening in her life? Did she believe that even if something awful happened because we live in this world filled with sin, God could give her the grace to go through that difficulty? Did she trust Him to weave even the bad things in her life into His plan so that good would be brought from it? Did she trust Him to give her peace and His presence in times of trouble?

Those are all questions that you need to ask yourself as you model Christian living in front of your daughter-in-law. Can your daughter-in-law tell that you are an authentic believer in Jesus Christ by how you react to life's curveballs? Do you show that you genuinely trust Him with the hurts of the past, the trials of the moment and the uncertainty of the future? Hopefully, your disposition is always one of trust in God no matter what is going on. That will speak more loudly and clearly to your daughter-in-law than anything you can say or do. Live life in front of her in such a way that will make her want to grow old to be just like you.

The best thing my mother-in-law has done for me is pray for me. I have never had to wonder if I was being prayed for.
—Anonymous

Be Honest About Yourself

The emboldened quotes throughout this book have included responses from a non-scientific survey completed by daughters-in-law from various parts of the country. These quotes concern the positive things that mothers-in-law have done. The goal in including them is for mothers-in-law to be encouraged by reading the affirming things that daughters-in-law have said about them. It gives us a clue to the heartbeat of our daughters-in-law and what has meaning for them. Perhaps by reading these quotes, you can be inspired to implement something brand new in your relationship with your daughter-in-law.

Another question that was incorporated into the survey was: "What does your mother-in-law do that drives you over the edge?" There is a lot to be learned by reviewing the responses to this question as well. Evaluating them may reveal to you an area in which you can improve in the relationship with your daughter-in-law. As you read these replies, be honest with yourself. Evaluate whether any of them ring true with your behavior in this complicated connection between mother-in-law and daughter-in-law.

I have categorized the list very loosely to enable you to better hone in on your area of weakness. Many of the responses would fit well in duplicate categories.

The Controlling Mother-in-law:

- She's always trying to push her ideas or views on us.
- Passive-aggressive when trying to interject about parenting my children, her grandchildren.
- Gives too much advice.

- She used to drive me crazy with taking over. She moved things in my cabinet, took things out of my pantry, freezer, etc. Now I love it when she does this. Please help me more! The biggest thing she did, though, that I will never forget, is when she was alone in our home and she snooped through important private papers. She admitted doing it, but never really apologized. We felt violated.
- My husband is the youngest of three boys and she babies him a lot. It drives me crazy and sometimes I wish she would just let him go!!
- Continues to baby her son and does everything for him.
- Treats my husband like a child.
- She can be quite controlling to my husband and to me. She is also very slow to apologize.

The Disrespectful Mother-in-law:

- She belittles me and finds things wrong with my house and with what I am doing.
- She doesn't respect me.
- Contradicts everything I say.
- She let me know that her four boys accomplished everything that was good in our marriages. We, (the daughters-in-law) were never credited for clean houses, well behaved children or any effort made to bring them to Christ.
- She will say bad things about me in front of other people.

The Insensitive Mother-in-law:

- Always talks about how wonderful, beautiful and smart her other daughters-in-law are.

- Tells stories ad-nauseum about her other grandkids when her own grandkids, mine, are right in front of her wanting attention. When we have her over, she calls her other sons.
- Relies on my hubby to be her fix-it, go-to guy, although this has improved. It used to stress out my husband and then me. I also hate it when she and my father-in-law put my hubby in the middle of their issues. They divorced a couple of years ago.
- Non-stop talking.
- She doesn't listen well.
- The way she still thinks her son is a child and that, no matter what, he can't do anything wrong.
- When we are in conversation, she interrupts me to talk about something that pertains nothing to the current conversation.
- Sometimes she compares my child, her grandchild, to other children in the family and praises her excessively. It's not necessary and it makes me feel uncomfortable and can create tension.
- She favors one of my sons over the other.
- She doesn't treat my daughter with the love she does for my sons.
- Smokes.
- Interrupts people when they are talking.

The Self-focused/Selfish Mother-in-law:

- She drinks a lot. She doesn't get drunk and pass out, but she puts it in her coffee in the morning.
- It's all about her. What she wants has to come first.

- She worries. Focuses on the problem, talks about it, fixates on it. Need I say more?
- Her irrational worry.
- She is very loud and dramatic at times.
- She always feels sorry for herself and blames her problems on others.
- She calls constantly, up to three and four times a day.
- She only calls when she needs something.

The Untrustworthy Mother-in-law:

- She shares our family issues with the extended family without asking first.
- Fails to take responsibility for her actions.
- She's a bit of a busy body and very opinionated.
- She constantly lies and then when caught in a lie she blames me!
- Gossips about other members of our family and other grandkids.

The Critical Mother-in-law:

- She doesn't call her son, my husband, on his birthday and says degrading, critical things about him and to him.
- Criticizes my kids or my parenting.
- I doubt my mother-in-law has any idea of the effect she has on my husband. He is faithful to call her every week in spite of the effect the calls have on him. It takes him literally 1 to 2 hours to recover from the criticism and guilt she piles on him. It's like she knows exactly where to aim the daggers. I *hate* the way she drains his emotional energy and tears him down.

- She has the knack of putting me down or criticizing me that only I pick up on. I feel so alone.

The Judgmental Mother-in-law:

- Judges my parenting.
- Refuses to babysit because she doesn't think that I should leave home without the kids. Seriously. She feels that my place is at home with the kids, and that if I want a haircut badly enough I'll take them along.
- She is always "sharing" articles from the newspaper about finances, child rearing, etc.

And happily, I will conclude the list of things that "drive daughters-in-law over the edge" with this response that one sweet daughter-in-law gave:

- Honestly, and it feels so good to be able to say this, *nothing!*

Do you see the recurring themes? Many of the subjects that were covered within the context of this book were named within these responses. Many redundant replies were omitted, but the fact that there were so many repetitions further illustrates that there are common issues that all mothers-in-law and daughters-in-law need to work through.

Did you see yourself in any of the situations that were listed? Pray and ask God to show you what you do that drives your daughter-in-law over the edge. Then reread the list again slowly and ask yourself as you do, "Am I guilty of that?" If you have an open heart and you read with a listening ear to God, He will be faithful to *gently* show you an area that can be improved upon.

Believe me, you would much rather have Him reveal something to you than to have your daughter-in-law reach the end of her rope and fire her frustration at you. Don't let it get to that point.

If there is a specific issue that you suspect may make her crazy, just ask her. If you don't pester or harangue her, but show a genuine desire to be your best, she will love you for it.

That final response gives me hope that the goal of being a great mother-in-law is attainable. God bless that aforementioned mother-in-law that did such a great job. I could kiss her right on the face.

One of the best things my mother-in-law ever did for me was to not have expectations that I need to do things like she did them. She has always been open about that. I can do and live how I want to. That was a great sense of relief. She told her boys the same so that they were not expecting their wives to be like their mom.
—Anonymous

Be Willing to Improve

Wouldn't it be great to know exactly what your daughter-in-law wanted or expected from you? Circumstances may not be right at this time to come out and ask her, but perhaps you can learn from some suggestions that other daughters-in-law have made about their mothers-in-law.

Following is a list of responses to the question, "What one thing could your mother-in-law do to improve your relationship?" Once again, I ask you to read them slowly and carefully consider if their ideas might work for the two of you. I have categorized them to illustrate the themes and greatest desires of daughters-in-law.

Invest In and Accept Me

- We could talk more.
- Communicate more.
- Invite me to spend personal time with her, aside from family time.
- Pursue having a relationship with me. If I didn't have kids, I don't think I'd have a single thing to talk to her about. She has no idea who I am as a person except that we're both Christians.
- Be friendlier.
- Communicate on a real basis, not so superficially. Ask, "What can I do to help?" and not, "How's the weather?"
- Be more willing to spend time with us at our house.
- I would love to have some alone, girl time with her.
- Be a better listener.
- Not be so selfish.
- Spend more personal non-family time with me.
- I wish she would call us more. I feel like she thinks that she is imposing. Every time she does call, we talk a long time and I feel the conversation is good. But there is just this, "I'm stepping back" kind of thing going on. I wish we could connect at least once a week.
- Call me more. Honestly. I should do the same.
- Spend more time together.
- Talk to me more.
- Be more interested in me as a person. Talk with me about my week, how my classes are going, how the kids are doing.
- Spend more time together.
- She could call and chat with just me.
- As odd as this may sound, I wish I didn't have to call her so much to get together. She feels like she's meddling

and gives us space, but I would like it if she called me occasionally to drop by or to go to lunch.
- I think it would improve our relationship if she and my father-in-law (or even just she alone) came to visit more often on weekends. They rarely come to visit. I think they come at most about twice a year. It would be great to have more dedicated time with them and have them see some of the kid's sports or arts performances.
- I lost my mom and my step-mom is distant (geographically and emotionally) so I would really enjoy a closer woman to woman interaction (with my mother-in-law) about the big and little things of life.
- Call more, write more, Skype more, and visit more. She doesn't show me that our relationship means something to her.
- Accept me.

Respect Us

- Allow us to parent our children ourselves.
- Be honest and understanding and <u>respectful.</u>
- Start treating me as if I were a grown woman.
- Realize that she has more than one wonderful son and that he has a lot to offer this world.
- Not gossip about me with the other two daughters-in-law.
- Not try to come between my husband and me.
- View us as adults.
- I wish she wouldn't dismiss my thoughts and opinions as if they didn't matter.
- Let go of her son and let him live his life.

- Quit buying knick knacks. (Apparently this mother-in-law has disregarded her daughter-in-laws wishes and those knick knacks keep a comin'.)

Be Grace-filled

- Be more loving and considerate.
- Understand that no one is perfect.
- Tone down the critical spirit. See the good things in the grandkids instead of picking on their hair, their weight, etc. And, accept gifts without making a critical comment.
- Be kinder to the kids when they acted up at her house.
- Keep her opinions about my children to herself.
- Compliment my mothering.
- I wish she would bring peace and forgiveness to the family, uniting divisions.

Invest in and Help With Grandchildren

- Come to see and spend more time with her grandkids.
- Put my kids first when she is with them.
- Offer to babysit.
- Spend more time with my son, her grandson.
- Stop criticizing our children.
- Probably just call once in a while to see if I need help with the kids and then offer to come to our house and help.
- Come around or call just to visit. Try to develop a relationship with her grandkids.
- Keep in better contact and help with my kids more.

Be Honest and Fair

- I've talked to her about this many times. I wish she would be more honest with me about her feelings about something (instead of grinning and bearing it when she doesn't feel like doing something), and letting me know what she thinks on an issue without being indirect. I think if she just came out and told me what she's feeling or thinking on an issue, we could just have a discussion about things right then and there and clear the air on things that she feels we should or shouldn't be doing.
- One thing she could do to improve our relationship would be to be more open and honest about things instead of pretending that everything is okay. She really is harboring bitterness and hurt and doesn't let me know. Instead she talks to her daughters about problems that she has with me. (NOT okay with me.)
- I would like her to work through issues and conflict directly.
- Believe that her son is not always perfect!
- Perhaps be a little more open to change, have a willingness to try new things and venture from her routine.

Be a Jesus Follower

- She could accept Jesus and me.
- Accept Jesus as her Savior! No really! Other than that, she is great and I can't think of anything.

And finally the answer that every mother-in-law would like to claim:

- Nothing. She has never been in the middle of our marriage! She is there for us when we need her but never too close.

We have addressed many of the things that these daughters-in-law found objectionable in previous chapters. The striking thing about this list is the number of daughters-in-law whose responses reveal that they long to have a real relationship with their mothers-in-law. They are just waiting for their mothers-in-law to reach out to them and show love and an interest in them and not just their husbands or children. Often daughters-in-law are floundering and struggling with the cares of life much more than we realize. There is nothing that they would like more than for someone who has been where they are to come alongside them and encourage them. Young daughters-in-law are yearning for role models and mentors. They see that potential in their mothers-in-law.

The problem is that mothers-in-law have had a bad rap as meddlers and even witches for so long that many have backed away from their son and daughter-in-law and have taken the hands-off approach. The feedback from this sampling of daughters-in-law reveals a different perspective than the traditional conventional wisdom. They desire to have a meaningful relationship with their mothers-in-law.

Why not take a risk and give it a try, mother-in-law? Begin giving your daughter-in-law a call on a regular basis. Inquire about her first and how she is doing before you inquire about your son and the kids. Ask if she would like to go to lunch, to a craft show or go shopping with you. If you really want to make her pass out, you arrange and pay for the babysitter. Reach out in some way to show genuine interest in your daughter-in-law with no strings attached. Do it solely for the purpose of affirming her and loving her. Treating her with that kind of attention, care and respect will naturally lead to a closer relationship with her.

But, if it doesn't, then what do you do? We'll talk about that in the next chapter.

I am so blessed by my mother-in-law. She is one of the most thoughtful people I know. I would say the best thing she has done for me is that every time we have had to move (which was more often in our early marriage) my mother-in-law has used her sewing skills to make me new custom window treatments for each new home in which we have lived. She takes me shopping for fabric, lets me pick whatever I like and then makes me beautiful window treatments for my new home. It has always made each new place we have lived in feel like home and is a way she has always showed love for me.
—Anonymous

Chapter 8

Now That We Are Friends

> "A man [or woman] that hath friends must shew
> himself [or herself] friendly: and there is a friend
> that sticketh closer than a brother [or sister]."
> (Proverbs 18:24 KJV)

One way to enhance your relationship with your daughter-in-law is to give her gifts of significance and meaning. If her "love language" is receiving gifts, you will hit a homerun by using this way to build the relationship between the two of you. Even if it is not her primary love language, who doesn't like to receive a gift especially if it has deep meaning attached to it? You must keep your goal in mind, dear mother-in-law. Your goal is not to change your daughter-in-law. Your goal is to love her and establish an enduring friendship with her.

Before giving any gift that has spiritual significance there are a couple of things that need to be considered. First, is your daughter-in-law a believer in Jesus Christ? If she is not, pray diligently and ask for the discernment of the Holy Spirit before you give her any of the suggested gifts. The point of doing this is to establish a long and lasting positive relationship with her not alienate her.

If your daughter-in-law is a Christ follower, pray and seek guidance as to which gift of spiritual significance you should give her. Ask for God's perfect timing as to when it should be given. No matter how much your daughter-in-law loves Jesus, if she is overwhelmed by the cares of life, a gift of spiritual significance *can* feel like a weight, or a burden, one more thing that she has to do to meet your expectations or to live up to the "Christian daughter-in-law" she probably really wants to be. If you pray, God will give you a sense about whether you should give her one of the items listed below and when they should be given.

Now let's get started talking about the fun stuff.....gift giving!

Bible

One of my favorite gift ideas is something that I saw a former Pastor of mine give to his son. He purchased a Bible for him and had his son's name engraved on the front. Instead of giving it to him right away, he kept the Bible and read it through himself and underlined his favorite verses, wrote sermon notes in it and even put messages in the margins for his son such as, "Son, pay close attention to this verse! I struggled at this point and I don't want you to do the same." At a significant time in his son's life, he gave it to him. Can you imagine what a blessing it was for that son to have such a personal, meaningful gift from his father? It is something that he will always treasure.

A mother-in-law could certainly do the same for her daughter-in-law. What better way for your daughter-in-law to really know you and see your heart than to give her a gift that reflects what has importance and value that lasts long after your life? This gift must be given in humility and with the right spirit, however. If it is done for any other reason, such as preaching to her or trying to change her behavior, your daughter-in-law will see through it in a moment and the gift could do more harm than good. Only the Holy Spirit can win someone to Himself or can change a person's behavior. As much as we would sometimes like to be, we are not our daughter-in-law's Holy Spirit. Our job is to pray for our daughters-in-law and to model the very attitudes of Jesus Himself.

We gave our children a variation of this gift when they got married. By the grace of God our sons' new mothers and fathers-in-law to be were wonderful believers in Jesus Christ. We parents wanted to give our children something to represent our faith and something that would act as a symbol that signified us passing the "baton of faith" from us to them. We purchased a Bible for the boys and their new wives and had their names engraved on the front of it. Instead of us all reading through that Bible, each parent wrote them a letter on one of the four different blank pages in the front. We met with them one hour before the wedding in the chapel. (Yes. The guys *did* see the brides before the wedding.) It was a precious and intimate time between the four parents and the bride and groom. We presented them with that Bible and told them that by doing so we were now sending them off to run the race of faith in their own new little family. We then were able to pray with them and ask God to help them live by the very words we were handing over to them. Then, we had to go fix our makeup because of all the boo-hooing. But, it is a memory that I cherish!

My heart was happy when we visited Chris and Holly soon after they were married. We walked into their new apartment and there was that Bible displayed prominently as we walked in the door. That Bible means even more now to my daughter-in-law,

Holly because her daddy has since gone to heaven. She has more reason than ever to value it as a precious gift.

The best thing that my mother-in-law has done for me is that she frequently tells me how thankful she is that God brought me into her son's life.
—Anonymous

Ebenezer

Before you let that weird word turn you off, let me explain. I love the hymn, "Come Thou Fount", but I have to admit that I was completely flummoxed every time I sang that last verse that says, "Here I raise my Ebenezer..." What in the world is an Ebenezer and why would I want to raise it? While reading my Bible one day I ran across the same word in I Samuel 7. The context is that the Israelites found themselves face to face with the dreaded and feared Philistines again. Verses 10 through 12 state: "While Samuel was sacrificing the burnt offering, the Philistines drew near to engage Israel in battle. But that day the LORD thundered with loud thunder against the Philistines and threw them into such a panic that they were routed before the Israelites. The men of Israel rushed out of Mizpah and pursued the Philistines, slaughtering them along the way to a point below Beth Car. Then Samuel took a stone and set it up between Mizpah and Shen. He named it Ebenezer, saying, 'Thus far has the LORD helped us.'"

The Ebenezer was called the stone of help. Its purpose was to remind the Israelites that God had been faithful to them. When they looked at that stone, they would remember what God had done and how He had helped them in the past against a dreaded enemy and that He could be trusted and would help them again. Over and over in God's word He instructs us to "remember" what He has done. Remembering encourages our spirits that God came through for us in the past and He will come through for us again. He can be trusted.

> "You will have these tassels to look at and so you will *remember* all the commands of the LORD, that you may obey them and not prostitute yourselves by going after the lusts of your own hearts and eyes." (Numbers 15:39)

> "*Remember* the day you stood before the LORD your God at Horeb, when he said to me, 'Assemble the people before me to hear my words so that they may learn to revere me as long as they live in the land and may teach them to their children.'" **(Deuteronomy 4:10)**

> "But *remember* the LORD your God, for it is he who gives you the ability to produce wealth, and so confirms his covenant, which he swore to your forefathers, as it is today." (Deuteronomy 8:18)

> "I *remember* the days of long ago; I meditate on all your works and consider what your hands have done." (Psalm 143:5)

> "*Remember* the wonders he has done, his miracles, and the judgments he pronounced…" (1 Chronicles 16:12)

And just in case we didn't get it, God has David's exact words repeated again in Psalm 105:5:

> "*Remember* the wonders he has done, his miracles, and the judgments he pronounced..." (Psalm 105:5)

> "*Remember* the former things, those of long ago; I am God, and there is no other; I am God, and there is none like me." (Isaiah 46:9) (emphasis added in all of the verses listed above)

Having visual aids is the easiest way to help us "remember." As we discussed this portion of scripture in Bible study one evening, one of the ladies came up with an idea to make an Ebenezer to give as a gift that would effectively serve as a tangible way to remember what God has done.

There are many variations as to how an Ebenezer can be constructed, but the few components needed are a clear container such as a glass bowl or cylinder, some smooth river rocks, a pillar candle and a sharpie pen. I usually go to a discount store and purchase a large, shallow glass bowl. The pillar candle is placed in the middle of the bowl and is surrounded by smooth river rocks that are at least 1 ½ inches across. You want them big enough that you can write on them. I usually tie some raffia around the candle and slip a sharpie pen between the raffia and the candle. I type on a piece of paper I Samuel 7:12,

> "Then Samuel took a stone and set it up... He named it Ebenezer, saying, 'Thus far the LORD has helped us.'"

Then punch a hole in the corner of it and thread the raffia through it before tying it around the candle. As God answers prayers the answers can be written on the rocks and placed in the bowl as a reminder. I leave mine out on an end table so that anyone coming into my home can see it. My grandchildren love to see their names written on the rocks and when they visit they often look in the bowl to make sure that their rock is still there. Just having an Ebenezer in my home reminds me, my children and grandchildren and even guests that God hears and answers prayer. When giving an Ebenezer as a gift, I have found that it is a good idea to write on the first rock so that the receiver of the gift "gets" how it is to work.

My youngest daughter-in-law, Nicole, had been struggling for years with endometriosis and desperately wanted to have a baby. To tell the truth, we didn't know if that would ever happen. We prayed and God in His mercy gave us a new beautiful grandson. You can be sure his name and the date of his birth are written on a rock! We will forever be grateful that God heard our prayers and allowed little Britton to be born. Britton was blessed too, whether he realizes it yet or not, because he got Nicole as a mommy. Someday he will look in that bowl and see the rock with his name on it we will be able to tell him how he is an answer to our prayers.

My mother-in-law has been such a great emotional supporter. I have been through two miscarriages and one high risk pregnancy. She has cheered me on through all of that reminding me how big my God is and how much He is holding me in His hands.
—Anonymous

Spiritual Heritage Video

I was blessed enough to have my godly grandmother until I was nearly 50 years old. We were kindred spirits and I loved her dearly. Not long before she died, I got the idea of preserving her spiritual story as well as her life story. This is when VHS cameras were still the thing. I visited her home one day, set up the camera on a tripod and then plopped down beside her and interviewed her. I asked how she met my grandfather, what life was like in the Great Depression, and most importantly, how she and my grandfather came to know Jesus personally. How had Jesus made a difference in their lives? It wasn't long after I taped that interview that she died. That account of my grandmother's testimony in her owns words is precious to me now. My husband has graciously transferred her VHS story onto a DVD to be preserved even longer. Now I have grandchildren of my own who have access to the spiritual account of their great, great grandmother. They can see and hear the rich heritage that they have in Jesus Christ.

Why not make a DVD or Spiritual Heritage Video to give to your daughter-in-law? This would give you one more opportunity to tell her in a lasting way how much you love her. If you have godly relatives that are older than you, you can interview and record them first. Then you can have someone interview you or both you and your husband or you can interview each other. If your husband is not a believer in Jesus Christ, don't let that stop you. You can always do a monologue into the camera and tell your son and daughter-in-law the things that you really want them to know about you and your faith.

Perhaps there is nothing that you would like more than to do something like this for your son and daughter-in-law, but they have never placed their faith in Christ and this would be of little or no value to them. Do it anyway.....just don't give it to them yet. There are a couple of things that you can do with it. First, you can wait for that exciting day that you have been praying toward for many years when they do accept Christ as the most important thing in their lives. Or, you can tell them that you have made a DVD of your life story and the things that you value most in life and you have a copy for them if they should ever want it. If they are hostile to even that, you could store it in your home to be found when you are gone. That sounds morbid but if God wants them to find it and have it, He will make that happen.

The hardest part of creating this gift for your daughter-in-law is just doing it. The temptation is to think that you'll always have the time later. It is so easy to put off. I am so grateful that I didn't put off interviewing my grandmother. Wouldn't you have loved for your mother-in-law to give you a gift of deep meaning like this?

My mother-in-law accepts and loves me unconditionally. She isn't judgmental.
—Anonymous

Blessing Box

One of the great privileges that we have as mothers-in-law is to be a sign post or an arrow that always points our daughters-in-law to Christ and His work. We do that by our lifestyle, our speech and even in some of the gifts that we give. We want to constantly reinforce biblical principles without being preachy.

Preachy doesn't work; in fact it repels instead of compels. What is compelling is a winsome, joy-filled life. There is nothing that can make you more filled with joy than to recount the blessings and goodness of God. There are a couple of gifts that can help you do that. The first is the Blessing Box.

The Blessing Box is easily and cheaply constructed. It is made from an empty oatmeal box and decorated with scrapbook paper or a cross stitched picture. Mine has the words Blessing Box on the outside with stickers of crosses and some Bible verses. Cut a hole in the top like you would a piggy bank. Make it big enough to slip pieces of paper through the hole. If given as a gift, also include several slips of paper with it. Every time something good happens to you or any member of your family, write that good thing on a piece of the paper and put it into the blessing box. God is the giver of *every* good gift. The Bible says that, "Every good and perfect gift is from above, coming down from the Father of the heavenly lights, who does not change like shifting shadows." (James 1:17)

This type of gift helps us to refocus from the created to the Creator and from the made to the Maker. It can cause us to look for God in our days and to be aware when we have had a "God sighting." So often God does a marvelous thing and its impact is diluted as it washes into all of the other happenings of our day. If we get into the habit of looking for God and recording His blessings, we are made more aware of His activity in our lives. It is just another of those techniques to make us intentional in our worship of Him.

I have an acquaintance that has a Blessing Box and it is kept in a prominent place in her home. She keeps a stack of white slips of paper beside her Blessing Box for anyone in the household to write on when something good happens to them. It is absolutely forbidden for anyone to look into that Blessing Box until

Thanksgiving Day. On that day after the turkey dinner, they do not run to take a nap or watch the football game. It is on that one day each year that they open their Blessing Box. The first person opens the box and pulls out one piece of paper and reads it aloud then passes it on and on around the table until every piece has been read. She told me that sometimes they sit at that table for up to two hours after the meal laughing and crying and remembering things long ago forgotten that God had done for them in the last year. What a celebration and day of Thanksgiving that is for their whole family! God must really enjoy it too.

Why not bless your daughter-in-law with a Blessing Box? This gift can be given with a note explaining how to use it. When your daughter-in-law needs a word of encouragement, she can open up the Blessing Box and see that God has been working and He does see her and care for her *or* she can wait for Thanksgiving.

My mother-in-law is the most generous person I know; always giving to others and always willing to help me in the kitchen and she will be 82 this year! She has the most energy of anyone I know and never passes judgment on anything I do except to give compliments which I don't deserve. She's the best!
—Anonymous

God Hunt Journal

Another gift that can be given to your daughter-in-law that will direct her attention to the goodness of God is a God Hunt Journal. Purchase a beautiful blank journal. Write a letter to your daughter-in-law on the first page and explain that this is a book in which she can record her blessings. Challenge her to find one good thing a day to write in her journal and explain that the point is for her to look for God and be hunting for His work throughout the regular routine of life. This is just one more tool to get us looking for God sightings rather than bogged down in the horrible or the mundane of life.

Be aware, however, that this type of gift has the potential of feeling like work to your daughter-in-law. There is another way to give the God Hunt Journal that can bless without giving her something else to do. Purchase a beautiful blank journal and once again, write the purpose on the first page. Instead of giving it to your daughter-in-law to fill out, you look for God sightings and His "good and perfect gifts" and you record them each day in the journal. When it is full or at the end of a year, give the journal to your daughter-in-law so that she can have a record of God's work in your life. Sharing your God Hunt journal is a great way to model a life of gratitude and praise for your daughter-in-law. You are mentoring without even being in her presence.

After having our daughter, my mother-in-law came and helped me out for a week. During the first month of my daughter's life we moved and my mother-in-law helped me pack my whole house. Not everyone has a relationship like we do and I feel beyond blessed to have a relationship full of laughter, tears and long conversations.
—*Anonymous*

Faithbooking

Scrapbookers will love this way to give a gift of significance. Faithbooking is scrapbooking with a twist. Wikipedia defines it as, "a creative expression of a family's spiritual journey, values and events that are captured in scrapbooks, diaries or journals that combine the use of photographs, decorated papers, scripture, thoughts, prayers, blessings, stories and embellishments such as buttons, ribbon and other creative art media. The goal of faithbooking is to creatively preserve and tell a story about how a family grows spiritually." The different ways that your Faithbook can be designed are as vast and varied as your imagination.

One way to put together a Faithbook is to concentrate on one spiritual event such as a baby dedication or a baptism where many pictures are taken. That event can be the theme of the entire book. Preserving that sacred moment and sharing that gift with your daughter-in-law will be giving her a gift of your time and your talents. I'm sure that it will be especially appreciated because most young mothers are not able to carve time out of their busy schedule to do a project of this kind.

Another way to construct a Faithbook that is meaningful is to pick favorite Bible verses and choose pictures that are compatible with each verse. Can't you just see a picture of your daughter-in-law's children, your precious grandchildren, accompanied by this verse?

> "Children are a gift from the LORD; they are a reward from him." (Psalm 127:3 NLT)

I read this verse the night before our oldest son left for college when I was in mourning over the end of my day to day mothering. I underlined it and put a note beside it in my Bible so that I would never forget it. A picture of my son unloading his things from our car and moving into the dorm room would be perfect on a page with this scripture beside it and a sentence or two of why this particular verse was chosen.

Another verse from Psalm 127 that would work well on a page that has a picture of one's home is:

> "Unless the LORD builds the house, it's builders labor in vain." (Psalm 127:1)

Or, on the same subject:

> "But as for me and my household, we will serve the LORD." (Joshua 24:15b)

A few more verses to spur your imagination and get your creative thoughts flowing are:

> "The glory of young men is their strength." (Proverbs 20:29a)

This verse is perfect for a page that has a picture of your son or grandson participating in an athletic event.

> "How good and pleasant it is when brothers [or brothers and sisters] live together in unity." (Psalm 133:1)

A sibling page would be a great place to include this scripture.

> "One generation will commend your works to another, they will tell of your mighty acts." (Psalm 145:4)

A multi-generational picture would make this scrapbook page complete.

On your pages dedicated to Christmas photos, this scripture of praise that the angels sang at Christ's birth would make them beautiful and pages of praise.

> "Glory to God in the highest, and on earth peace to men on whom his favor rests." (Luke 2:14)

I will conclude with two ideas before you take off and start scrapping your own. The first: Writing or typing an answer to prayer on each page and placing a photo that represents your answer can make a lasting treasure for future generations of your family. Your children and grandchildren will have tangible evidence that their mother-in-law/grandmother prayed and God answered that prayer. What a faith booster and what a way to honor God and give Him the glory for the things He has done in your life!

Second, don't feel boxed in by the idea that a verse or answer to prayer has to have a themed picture along with it. Perhaps you may just want to compile your favorite verses in your Faithbook and place beside them beautiful drawings or photographs of nature. There is no limit nor are there boundaries to what you can do as you design your Faithbook.

There are many sites available to you on the internet that can help you get additional designs and materials for your Faithbook. Pinterest is loaded with ideas. Simply type, "Faithbooking" on the search line and page ideas, scriptures and boards will pop up to give you inspiration. Googling the word Faithbook will lead you to many resources to help you create your book in a way that will make it a very special gift to your daughter-in-law. A helpful website that I discovered is www.faithfullyyours.net which includes faithbooking articles, tutorials, a gallery of completed pages, scripture concordance, and a section entitled, Scrapbook Ministry. There are books listed on Amazon, one of which is entitled, *Faithbooking and Spiritual Journaling: Expressions of Faith Through Art* by Sharon Soneff. If scrapbooking is your thing, get started and give a gift that will have a lasting and meaningful impact.

What is the best thing about my mother-in-law? It's hard to narrow it down to one thing. She's someone I can talk to. She is honest about things. She gives great advice and she accepts my opinion and respects me as a mother.
—*Anonymous*

Write Your Daughter-in-law a Letter

Writing can feel like a burden to me so this gift would not come as easily for me as it does for a dear friend of mine who is a gifted writer. In fact, she is in the process of publishing her twenty-first novel. Because writing is second nature to her, she decided to write each of her children a letter every month. She included all of the things that were capturing their attention that month, whether it was activities at school or spiritual struggles. She kept the letters so that she could give them to her children at a significant time in their lives. Those letters are a historical and spiritual account of what took place in those kid's lives.

This wonderful thing that she has done for her children could just as easily be done for your daughter-in-law. Write her a letter monthly or quarterly or on her birthday or anniversary recounting how much you love her or some quality that you see in her that means so much to you. You could include the happenings in your lives since the last time that you wrote or incorporate current events. These letters could be given to her immediately or saved for a significant time like the birth of her first baby or on her ten year anniversary. Letter writing is a lost art. It takes time and effort. That is one reason why it will be so appreciated. The other reason is that it will reinforce to your daughter-in-law that you love and value her!

I had a great mother-in-law! Even though she didn't understand our decision to have 10 kids and homeschool all of them, she was supportive. She had 7 kids and knew the hard work that went into caring and raising them. She also made each of her grandchildren feel so very special! She always put others before herself and didn't want people to fuss over her. She was a strong encouraging woman, and now as of Monday is rejoicing in heaven with Jesus.
—*Anonymous*

Prayer Shawl

Perhaps you are not a Scrapbooker or a writer but you love to knit or crochet. A Prayer Shawl would be the perfect gift for you to make for your daughter-in-law. The word "shawl" conjures up feelings of warmth, comfort and security. A gift of this kind would hopefully convey those same feelings. The shawl could be given to her on a special occasion, at Christmas time, her birthday or if she has been going through a difficult time. The key word to this gift though, is "prayer." Pray before you begin and pray for your daughter-in-law as you create it. When you present it to her, let her know that it is a gift that comes with prayer woven through every stitch. When she feels lonely, abandoned, misunderstood, frustrated or even cold in her spirit, she can wrap that shawl around her and know that she is loved, deeply cared about and prayed for by her husband's mother.

I have included a pattern for a simple crocheted Prayer Shawl in the appendix. There are many sites on the internet with much more elaborate and intricate patterns for prayer shawls than the one that I have included. Once again, Pinterest had the most prayer shawl patterns of any site that I found. Both knit and crochet patterns are included as well as lovely sayings and cards that can be made to accompany the shawl that you make. Another site devoted to prayer shawls is www.shawlministry.com. It includes free patterns as well as a photo gallery and a section entitled, Stories and Inspiration. Another place to go to for patterns is www.amazon.com. There you will find a book for sale entitled, *The Prayer Shawl Companion: 38 Knitted Designs to Embrace, Inspire and Celebrate Life.* It is available in paperback and is given a rating of 4 ½ stars out of 5.

When you give your daughter-in-law a Prayer Shawl, you are also giving her a gift of your time and especially the gift of prayer. She will have a tangible, physical reminder that she has a mother-in-law that loves, cares about her and prays for her.

The best thing my mother-in-law ever did for me was that she was very supportive in our relationship.
—Anonymous

Life Bible Verse(s)

When our boys were young, I decided that I should have a life verse for each of them. I had in mind that I was looking for a verse or a few verses that characterized them; verses that I could use to pray for them. I rolled the idea around in my head and kept it simmering just under the surface of my mind as I read my Bible and had my devotions each day. I would even go for a period of time when it didn't come to my conscious thoughts. I knew that God would let me know what verse or verses would be right for each son in His time.

A friend of mine shared with me one day a passage from Proverbs 2 that she had been meditating upon. I reread the scripture and just *knew* that those verses best suited and represented our son, Jon. They were going to be the ones that I attached to him. I could pray those verses for him and put his name into them knowing they epitomized him. Those verses are:

> *1 My son, if you accept my words*
> *and store up my commands within you,*
> *2 turning your ear to wisdom*
> *and applying your heart to understanding—*
> *3 indeed, if you call out for insight*
> *and cry aloud for understanding,*
> *4 and if you look for it as for silver*
> *and search for it as for hidden treasure,*
> *5 then you will understand the fear of the LORD*
> *and find the knowledge of God.*
> *(Proverbs 2:2-5)*

Jon was the type of kid who loved to study and learn. He would memorize all of the cards in our Trivial Pursuit game just because he liked to have knowledge. The fact that he beat us every time was also a powerful motivator. He has been very spiritually sensitive since he was little and has striven to know and understand God. Those verses fit him. I have a similar story for each of our other sons, but I share this with you to give you an idea of how it worked for me as I searched.

Awareness dawned on me that I should also choose a verse or verses for each of my daughters-in-law. I could put their names in those verses and pray them regularly for the girls. I have found a verse for Holly and for Bekah and am still looking and praying for God to lead me to just the right verse for Nicole.

Choosing and praying a scripture just for your daughter-in-law is an incredible gift. You begin by asking God to lead you to a verse or verses that characterize her. Consider her qualities, likes, personality and the major events that have taken place in her life. For example, the verses that I found for our first daughter-in-law, Holly are from Isaiah 43:2-3.

Holly is a people person; she's a musician, an athlete and many other wonderful things. In the last few years, however she has suffered with some physical problems including two back surgeries that have forced her to give up most of the activities in which she excels and that she enjoys. It has been a trying and difficult time for her. Her faith in Christ remains the bedrock of her life and that's why I knew the verses from Isaiah were for her.

> *2 When you pass through the waters,*
> *I will be with you;*
> *and when you pass through the rivers,*
> *they will not sweep over you.*

> *When you walk through the fire,*
> *you will not be burned;*
> *the flames will not set you ablaze.*
> *³ For I am the LORD your God,*
> *the Holy One of Israel, your Savior*
> *(Isaiah 43:2-3)*

When I shared these verses with Holly and told her that these were the special verses that God had given me for her, she looked at me and said, "This means more to me than you will ever know." It was worth finding that verse for her.

Our second daughter-in-law, Bekah has always had a heart for people of other cultures. She is a deep thinker, she's caring and she is willing to give up creature comforts so that she can share Jesus with others. When she and Jon first really noticed one another they were on a Mission Trip to Mexico. Now they serve together in Ethiopia. Bekah has sacrificed and worked to put Jon through four years of Medical School, five years of Residency and then she surrendered even more by selling their home and nearly all of their possessions to move to Africa. Is it any wonder that I knew that the following verse was for her? This verse embodies Bekah and her life.

> "And everyone who has left houses or brothers or sisters or father or mother or children or fields for my sake will receive a hundred times as much and will inherit eternal life." (Matthew 19:29)

When I pray this scripture for Bekah, it is very similar to this: "Father, You know that Bekah has sold her home, her furniture, she's given up her career, and she rarely sees her extended family because she wants to serve You. Her sacrifice because of her devotion to You must bring such joy to Your heart. I pray that You will help her to know that Your smile is upon her and that she and Jon and the girls will receive a hundred times as many blessings. Thank you, Lord that they are going to inherit eternal life that is worth so much more than the things they've given up."

If you decide that finding a special verse is something that you would like to do for your daughter-in-law, don't panic if the Bible verse does not come to you right away. Continue to pray and the Holy Spirit will lead you to it. I still have not found the perfect verse for my third daughter-in-law, Nicole. She relishes being a Mommy and she is an excellent one. I believe that the verse will have something to do with that, but I will wait until God makes it clear.

How blessed your daughter-in-law will be when you tell her that God has led you to a portion of scripture that exemplifies her and that you pray it for her regularly. That is a gift that will reach past the end of this life and into forever!

The best thing my mother-in-law ever did for me was accept me from day one.
—Anonymous

Overwhelmed Yet?

Looking over this list of all of the gifts that you could give to your daughter-in-law can be totally daunting. No one can do all of this. I don't. Perhaps this word picture will be helpful to those whose minds are spinning.

Have you ever walked into a room in your home that was totally trashed? There were things dumped over, some sort of sticky liquid on the floor, clothes and stuff everywhere and dishes of moldy food under the sofa or bed? It's so bad that you are looking over your shoulder to see if the television cameras have shown up yet because you could be the next star of *Hoarding* on A and E. Your inclination is to turn right back around and walk out because the mess is just too overwhelming. It is hard to know even where to begin.

What would happen if you did not move or turn around to walk out but just bent over and picked up the closest thing to your foot and put that one thing away? Then you bent over again and picked up one more things and put that away. Before you know it, just by picking up one thing at a time and putting that away, you would have the room ready for habitation again and there would be no need for the cameras.

You can approach giving your daughter-in-law a spiritually significant gift in the same way. Just pick up the one thing that you *can* do. Choose one that works with your temperament and personality and that she would appreciate. By "picking up the one thing" and giving her the one gift that is doable for you, you will be building a bridge to a great relationship with your daughter-in-law. And what woman doesn't like to receive gifts?

She encouraged spending time alone with my husband, whether it was a walk, a picnic, a dinner out, or an overnight. All of those times enhanced our marriage which made us better parents. Those times alone would enhance the understanding of each other and our family.
—*Anonymous*

Non-Spiritual Gifts (That Will Make Her Love You Forever)

Not all meaningful gifts have a spiritual component. Often times a young wife and mom is so exhausted from the demands of her children and job and husband and the house that a spiritual gift is lost on her. What she really needs is a break.

House Exchange

Marie has her hands full as a nurse and mother to five children, four of whom are very active boys. Sometimes she gets overwhelmed and just plain weary with all of the noise and activity. A tremendous amount of energy is required to care for them. Her husband is great, but he has a full-time job too. Money is an issue, but they really needed time away for just the two of them. Marie's in-laws came to the rescue with a brilliant and, here's the best part, free plan. Their plan was to have a house exchange. Her mother and father-in-law live about an hour and a half away. Marie's mother-in-law cleaned her own house, baked some goodies and had the place looking comfy, warm and inviting. Her mother-in-law and father-in-law then drove to Marie's house and sent Marie and her husband, their son, off to occupy the in-law's home for the weekend. This single act of kindness and thoughtfulness accomplished every goal. It allowed grandma and grandpa to be with their grandchildren for a whole weekend. It allowed the kiddos to get to stay in their own beds, in their own environment with their own Xbox and their own friends. It allowed my worn out friends to have a weekend away alone together *at no cost*!!!

What do you think that did for the relationship between Marie and her mother-in-law? That was love in action. I asked Marie what she thought of her mother-in-law and she told me how much she loves her. I can imagine why. That mother-in-law is tuned in to the needs of her daughter-in-law and doesn't just speak about loving her but shows it by what she does.

Why not do a house exchange with your son and his wife? And don't forget to leave some chocolate on the pillow.

The best thing my mother-in-law ever did for me was ask me what I wanted to call her after my husband and I were married. She said that she had not been given any options when she was married and she didn't want me to experience the same thing. It was her desire that I be comfortable with my name for her.
—Anonymous

Surprise Meal in a Basket

Do you remember how hard it was to come up with meal ideas when you were first married? Do you remember how exhausted you were when you got home from work and there was still supper to prepare? It's likely that at least once a month you probably forgot to get something out of the freezer.

Your daughter-in-law is experiencing those kinds of days too. If you live in close proximity and you have knowledge that it has been a tough week or that she is going through a hard time, take a meal over in a basket *and leave it*. Don't stay. It is not an excuse for you to go to their house and hang out with them. The point is to love her and show her you care by an act of kindness. This is not something that should be done often or it will look like you don't think that she is doing a good enough job as a cook for your son. When done infrequently with the right motives, this can be another action that can build a bridge between you and your daughter-in-law.

The best thing my mother-in-law ever did for me was give me words of affirmation, basically telling me I have a patience and firmness with the kids and she admires that.
—*Anonymous*

Pamper Time

Sometimes the best gift to give our girls is one they pick themselves. That way you can never go wrong. A Starbuck's gift card tucked under a placemat after your kids have had you over for a meal can be a nice little surprise. If your daughter-in-law is not into coffee, find out what she does love and give her a gift card to that place. It doesn't have to be for a lot of money. The point is that you have listened to her to discover what she likes and you have actually gone to the trouble of purchasing a gift card for her.

That is really what our daughters-in-law want to know. Do we really listen to them? Do we really care about what they care about? Do we really love them? Remember our mantra? No one can resist anyone who loves them unconditionally.

I really appreciate my mother-in-law's faithfulness with birthday cards, Chinese New Year and Christmas cards (even though she doesn't celebrate it). The dollars aren't much but she prioritizes remembering us. She spent a long time picking out just the right card for my son's graduation.
—*Anonymous*

Chapter 9

When Nothing Seems to Work

> "You have heard that it was said, 'Love your neighbor and hate your enemy.' But I tell you, love your enemies and pray for those who persecute you, that you may be children of your Father in heaven."
> (Matthew 5:43, 44)

All Efforts Spurned

Leigh and John's son, Tim, went to college a thousand miles from home. Tim met and fell in love with a coed whose home was eight hundred miles beyond that. By his senior year in college, Tim and his girlfriend, Miranda became engaged. Leigh and John were excited to finally have a girl in the family and were glad that Tim seemed to be so blissfully happy with his bride-to-be. The distance prohibited Leigh and John from getting to know Miranda well. In their few meetings she was nice and extremely polite if not a little quiet.

Through the course of conversations and planning the wedding, Leigh observed the closeness of Miranda and her mother. There didn't seem to be much room or need for another woman in Miranda's life. Leigh was often left out or ignored and her feelings were hurt a few times throughout the wedding planning and preparation process. She decided that she was going to hang in there and try to build a relationship with her new daughter-in-law despite the fact that they would rarely see one another.

Soon after they were married, Tim was accepted to begin his PhD program at a university near Miranda's folks and a thousand miles away from his. He was extremely busy going to school and teaching so there was not much time to keep in contact with his mom and dad. It seemed as though Leigh was always the one who initiated the phone calls and communication. Miranda was busy with her career and her parents and she didn't reach out to her new mother-in-law.

A few years passed and things continued to cool between them. One day, however, Leigh and John got a phone call that most parents of married children love to get. They found out that they were going to be grandparents! They were overjoyed and rejoiced in the exciting news. Leigh purchased little outfits and mailed them to Tim and Miranda. After all, this was going to be her first grandchild; anyone would splurge in the same situation.

The day finally came for Leigh and John's first grandson to arrive. They were ecstatic and were willing to buy expensive plane tickets or do whatever they had to do to see that little guy. John and Leigh arranged to rent a place for one week right across the hall from their kids so they could have easy access to their new grandbaby and cram all the togetherness they could into the short time that they were able to be there. Leigh was aware things between she and Miranda were still awkward and strained. She didn't realize how bad things had become until she and John excitedly knocked on Tim and Miranda's door the day they arrived in town to see their new grandson. That fact was made quite clear when they *were turned away* from seeing their first grandchild because Miranda was having "special time with the baby." What? They had flown half way across the country to see their first grandchild and were turned away? Leigh and John waited across the hall all day long. After several hours, they were finally allowed to see their grandson. Leigh was beyond hurt at the disregard that her daughter-in-law and her son had for their feelings. Now what would become of the relationship between this mother-in-law and daughter-in-law or this couple and their son?

I can hear you mothers yelling from here, "What is the matter with their son that he would allow this kind of disrespectful behavior toward his mother and father?" That was my initial thought as well until I talked to another son whose wife treated his mother in the same manner. I asked him why he let his wife accept gifts, money, food and vacations from his parents while at the same time never allowing his folks to come to their house. In the twenty plus years that they were married, this woman never permitted her in-laws to stay all night in their home despite the fact that his parents lived out of state and had to travel to see them. In talking to me about his marriage, he said that he allowed some of the bad behavior to continue because he had to pick his battles and he knew that was one that he wasn't going to win. He was trying desperately just to hold his marriage together. Unfortunately, it didn't work and the marriage ended in divorce. That mother-in-law continues to love and pray for her ex-daughter-in-law.

Let's hope that in most situations a son would insist that his parents deserve time with the grandchildren and with them. However, in really difficult relationships the poor guy may just be trying to keep his marriage from dissolving. That's not to imply that it is right, but it may give a bit of understanding of his complicated circumstance.

I asked Leigh what she does to try to repair and rebuild the relationship with her daughter-in-law and what her advice would be to other mothers-in-law that are in similar situations. Her words to me were, "Never close the door. Always keep trying and always keep praying."

Unfortunately, we live in a fallen, broken world that is filled with the pain of damaged or broken relationships. Many daughters-in-law come into a marriage with years of hurt already deposited in their emotional bank. Her behavior may not be as much about you as it is about herself and the trunk of guilt, scars and shame that she has accumulated over the years and is dragging into the marriage. Her pain then becomes your pain when it affects your relationship with her or your son.

Whatever the reason for the strain between you and your daughter-in-law, God can use that situation for your good and His glory. That hurtful circumstance can result in accomplishing something in you that a smooth, seamless relationship could not. It *is* pain, though, and pain hurts, but that hurt can be the very thing that reveals your need for God and causes you to cling to Him. If you look, there is a gift for you buried in this hurtful situation and that is that you can know and serve God in a deeper way than you ever dreamed possible. Don't waste your sorrow. Allow God to use this as a pathway to your spiritual maturity.

As mothers we tend to be Miss Fix-its. We can become consumed with trying to change an undesirable situation and miss the lessons that God has for us right in the middle of that situation. It is not a bad thing to try to change your circumstance and make things better, but when you have done all that you can do, leave the rest in the very competent hands of Almighty God.

Our ultimate goal is to know Him. This awkward relationship can be a tool in which you can get to know Him better. Keep in mind that Jesus experienced hurt and rejection to a greater degree than we will ever know. He was rejected by the very world He came to save. He understands rejection. The rejection of your daughter-in-law and the sickening feeling that accompanies it is a reminder of what God will *never* do to you. God said in Deuteronomy 31:8, "The LORD himself goes before you and will be with you: he will never leave you nor forsake you. Do not be afraid; do not be discouraged." He won't leave you to suffer alone. You can trust the God that became a man and entered into our pain with us.

Gary Thomas said in his book *Authentic Faith*, "God doesn't offer us freedom from a broken world. Instead He offers us friendship with Himself as we walk through this fallen world. Those who persevere will find that this friendship is worth more, so very much more than anything this fallen world can offer." I know that you may not believe me right now, but if your relationship with your daughter-in-law never gets better, there are still sweet treasures to be discovered.

There is always hope, however if you have God. Don't write off your relationship. God can melt the hardest heart or change the most difficult circumstance. Dale Carnegie, writer, lecturer and developer of famous courses in self-improvement, reminds us that, "Most of the important things in the world have been accomplished by people who have kept on trying when there seemed to be no hope at all." Just don't allow the resolution of your difficulties with your daughter-in-law to become more consuming than your passion for God.

It is normal to feel hurt that you are not close to your daughter-in-law. It is totally understandable to be disappointed.

Any mother-in-law in a contentious relationship with her daughter-in-law would feel the same way. Being entangled in a touchy relationship is not how you always dreamed things would be when your son got married.

There are things that you can do to help you in a difficult relationship. Find a real friend in whom you can confide that is long on listening, short on giving advice and mute on telling others your business. Talk to older, experienced mothers-in-law and inquire as to how they handled difficult situations with their daughters-in-law. Get involved in Bible studies and seek strength from God's word and of course, pray. Finally, keep loving, keep living a life of integrity and making sure that your heart is right before God. Keep praying for her and for the situation and *never shut the door.*

My mother-in-law taught me how to love them [my in-laws] by showing her love to me. [She gave me] surprise lunches, unexpected gifts, and words of love and encouragement.
—Anonymous

When You Are Old and Gray

"Let us not become weary in doing good, for at the proper time we will reap a harvest if we do not give up."
(Galatians 6:9)

I wish I could say that reading this book will make you into the perfect mother-in-law. It won't. Unfortunately there has never been one. So please keep in mind as you strategize and begin implementing techniques that you have discovered, the goal to be perfect is unattainable. Before you throw your hands in the air and wonder why you should even try, be encouraged with this good news. When you realize your own inadequacy, you become dependent on God and His help and strength. If you could actually attain perfection you would have no need of God and would rely on yourself or your own talents and abilities instead of on Him. Being unable to be a perfect mother-in-law puts you in the optimum position to depend upon God for your help and strength. His resources are limitless. You couldn't be in better hands.

Your real goal should be to be the best mother-in-law that God can help you to be. With His help you can work to improve your relationship with your daughter-in-law. He can cause you to love her whether you ever see the fruit of your love or not. Dear mother-in-law, keep loving, keep giving, keep serving, and keep trying. Love her in such a way that when you come to the end of your life there will be no regrets on your part. *Never close the door on the relationship* with your daughter-in-law, and leave the rest in God's hands. He can handle it.

My prayer for you as you navigate these sometimes murky waters is: "Dear God, help these precious women to be the best imperfect mothers-in-law that they can be for their daughters-in-law, but especially for You. Help them to know that getting their daughters-in-law to change is not the answer, being best friends with their daughters-in-law is not the ultimate goal in life, even having all of their prayers answered concerning their daughters-in-law will not bring happiness in this life. YOU are the treasure. When they fully comprehend that You are the treasure Lord, they will have everything they need to be the mother-in-law that you created them to be. Amen."

Cheryl Oliver Pollock

We could always count on [my mother-in-law] to pray in time of need. She was diligent about studying the Bible. She often read to me some new revelation she had learned from her Bible study. She also loved to read Christian books and would pass on her favorites to me like, Christian Secrets of a Happy Life, and books on prayer by Richard Foster. This spiritual sharing truly affected my spiritual walk with Christ. My mother-in-law was a gift to my life. I am anxious to see [her] in heaven someday.
—Anonymous

Appendix

Easy Crochet Prayer Shawl Pattern

I have made many prayer shawls and will include my simple pattern for those who enjoy crocheting. You will need four skeins of 3.5 oz. yarn in your daughter-in-law's favorite color and a size J crochet hook. If you would like to make it just a bit more fancy, purchase 10 glass, metal or wood beads to be crocheted into one end.

Find the end of the skein and BEFORE YOU BEGIN TO CHAIN, thread all 10 beads onto the end of the yarn.

After they are threaded onto the yarn, slide them down several yards.

Chain 47.

The last three stitches will act as the first double crochet of the second row. Double crochet in the fourth chain from the end and continue double crocheting the rest of the 43 stitches to complete the second row.

Chain 3 to begin the third row. When you catch up to the beads, slide them down until you are ready for them. Double crochet in the fourth stitch from the end and complete the third row.

Row four: Repeat instructions for row three.

On row five, chain three, double crochet three stitches and then pull one of the beads all the way up against the crochet hook and crochet around it as if it were not there.

Double crochet four more stitches and pull up the next bead.

Continue this pattern across the entire row.

When you have completed row five, you will have the beads securely crocheted into the prayer shawl as a beautiful extra touch.

Continue the double crochet pattern back and forth until you have used three skeins of yarn.

It is at this point that I stop and cut the fringe for the shawl from the fourth skein so that I won't have to guess how much of the skein to use before I run out without enough yarn for fringe.

Cut five pieces of yarn each of which should be 15 inches long. That will make up one fringe bundle. You will need 44 bundles. That is the most tedious part of the entire project.

Use the yarn that is left on the fourth skein after the fringe bundles are made to continue crocheting the shawl.

When you have crocheted the remainder of the fourth skein, tie off the yarn.

Tie a fringe bundle of five strands of yarn every other stitch across each end of the shawl.

There will be 22 fringe bundles on each end.

The finished shawl will be approximately six feet long not counting the fringe. That is the perfect length for your daughter-in-law to wrap up in and feel very cozy and loved.

Made in the USA
Lexington, KY
12 September 2014